Tom Slemen's
MYSTERIOUS WORLD

© Tom Slemen 2003

Published by The Bluecoat Press, Liverpool
Book design by March Design, Liverpool
Printed by The Universities Press, Belfast

ISBN 1 904438 06 7

All rights reserved. No part of this publication may be reproduced, stored in a retrieval system, or transmitted in any form or by any means, electronic, mechanical, photocopying, recording or otherwise, without prior permission from the publisher.

Tom Slemen's
MYSTERIOUS
WORLD

The Bluecoat Press

Contents

Introduction	5
The Turin Shroud – Mediaeval Forgery or Paranormal Image?	6
Did Joan of Arc Escape the Flames?	11
The A38 Hitch-Hiker	16
The Boy from Nowhere	19
The Giant Spider of the Ukraine	26
Homer – Man, Woman or Committee?	29
Date with Death	32
The Brahan Seer	37
Who Was the Bard of Stratford?	40
The Ancient Ones	42
The Strange Solitary Scientist	46
Is There Intelligent Life on the Moon?	50
The Man Who Couldn't Be Hanged	58
What Was the Fate of Britain's Spy Diver?	61
The Tunguska Alien	66
Zodiac	72
The Riddle of the Russian Hell	78
The Frozen Woman	80
In Three Places at Once	83
Was Einstein's Brain Different from Everyone Else's?	87
The Man Who Led Two Lives	89
The Inner Voice	91
Beware the Ides of March	93
What Mr Butler Saw	96
The Cock Lane Ghost	101
The Berkeley Square Entity	110
The Coffins Are Restless Tonight	114
Haunted by His Future Wife	118
The Welsh Werewolf	122

Introduction

In this volume, I have brought together a fascinating and thought-provoking collection of incidents and accounts from my own extensive files on the paranormal.

In this technological age, it is tempting to think that we now fully understand our world – after all, we have split the atom, made human organ transplants commonplace, read the genetic code, walked on the surface of the moon, travelled at 32 times the speed of sound and created complex computers that can easily carry out 250 million floating point operations per second, and we have even cloned Dolly the sheep.

But, despite these breakthroughs, we are still underachievers in other areas. We still bury and burn refuse rather than recycling it, and no one has yet found an environmentally friendly way to dispose of nuclear waste. Because of the industrialised nations' careless disregard for the environment, we have now inherited acid rain, ozone depletion, global warming, pollution on a massive scale, BSE and many more ecological problems.

On the exploration front, man has made six brief visits to the moon, but there are still many unexplored regions on our own planet. The Amazon Basin, the Poles, Alaska, Greenland, the Himalayas, the impenetrable jungles of New Guinea, Micronesia, and the highlands of Guiana, are still largely unexplored.

When we take these facts into consideration, it becomes clear that man still inhabits a world where maps and scientific theories are still incomplete; a world where ships and people and planes can still disappear without trace. There is so much on this earth – and off it – that is still unknown to man, and only a fool or a devout sceptic can fail to realise this.

In this collection of stories, I invite you to marvel with me at the mysteries which I have uncovered, from all ages and many different parts of the world. Each story will challenge your preconceptions and fire your imagination. And, as ever, I leave it up to you, the reader, to make up your own mind.

Tom Slemen
February 2003

THE TURIN SHROUD – MEDIAEVAL FORGERY OR PARANORMAL IMAGE?

After the Crusades, the wandering mendicant friars of Europe were like travelling salesman dealing in holy relics. Pieces of the Virgin's gown, fragments of crusts from the Last Supper, and even the knuckle bones of St Peter were peddled in every town. Reformers such as John Calvin and Martin Luther condemned the religious pedlars, but relics were big business. One critic of the day calculated that a replica of Noah's Ark could have been built with all the pieces of Christ's cross that had been sold to the gullible!

The Roman Catholic Church also condemned the relic merchants, and at the end of the nineteenth century, the Vatican issued a proclamation stating that: 'No relic, be it the most sacred in Christendom, can be regarded as authentic'. Even today, 32 'genuine' nails from Christ's cross, and three corpses of Mary Magdalene, are venerated around the world!

One of the most famous alleged relics is the burial cloth, or shroud, of Christ. Its early history is unknown, but the cloth was said to have been kept hidden for three hundred years after the crucifixion of Jesus, during the Christian persecutions. It was later acquired by the treasury of the Byzantine rulers of Constantinople. When the city was sacked in 1204, the Crusaders took the shroud to France, where it was kept at Besançon Cathedral, in the province of Doubs.

After narrowly being destroyed by a fire at the cathedral in 1349, the shroud was presented to the Dukes of Savoy in 1432. Another fire almost consumed the cloth at the ducal palace, but the flames failed to do any serious damage to the strange image of a man displayed on the shroud. The relic was taken to Turin, where the dukes had another residence, and there it has been kept since 1578. Every 33 years (the supposed age of Christ when he died), the Holy Shroud of Turin was put on display for the thousands of pilgrims who flocked to see it.

Scientists and most learned men in the nineteenth century naturally regarded the cloth as a pathetic forgery, and who could blame them? Science and the Church were moving in separate directions – Darwin had virtually proven that man had evolved from the same ancestors as the primates, and the pieced-together fossil remains of dinosaurs were painting a very different picture of the earth's past from the halcyon tales of Eden in the Book of Genesis.

Then, in 1898, a rectangular strip of linen, four metres long by one metre wide, sent out shockwaves that were to rock the religious and scientific world for the next century. That year, Secondo Pia, a Turin photographer, was commissioned to take the first photographs of the cloth, which was said to be the burial cloth of Jesus of Nazareth.

On the so-called Shroud of Turin all Secondo could see was a ghostly, faint, yellowish-brown imprint of a human figure who was naked and bearded. Secondo thought nothing of the photographic subject – until he was developing the plates in his darkroom. On the plates was the crisp image of a man, not in negative – but in positive. Secondo was so shocked by the revelation, that he dropped one of the plates. The Shroud of Turin was apparently a photographic negative.

At the French Academy of Sciences, Dr Yves Delage, a brilliant physicist and zoologist, made it his goal to discover how the negative image of a man could have been put on the cloth, centuries before the advent of photography. Delage spent three years on his project, and tried a myriad of ways to reproduce an identical shroud. He employed fine artists, but even the most skilled ones could not recreate the image's exact tones. The artists even experimented with mediaeval pigments, but had to call it a day in the end. Delage was forced to admit defeat, but he thought that the formation of the image may have had something to do with the way the Jews of Christ's time treated their dead. Their most frequently used burial ointments were myrrh and aloes, and Delage conjectured that these compounds, reacting with the urea given off in sweat by a dead body, may have caused an ammonia-based substance which stained the shroud.

Delage, who was renowned for being an agnostic and a militant anti-Catholic, caused quite a stir when he presented his findings to the Academy of Sciences in 1902. He told his colleagues that the cloth had indeed been Christ's shroud, but this claim was greeted by an uneasy silence. His findings were rejected and the Academy even took the unprecedented step of refusing to print Delage's carefully presented evidence in their minutes.

For 30 years, Delage's findings were only discussed by learned men in private – none of them would go on record to discuss the shroud. It was left to another Frenchman – Dr Pierre Barbet – a forensic pathologist, to take a further look into the controversial relic, this time from a medical viewpoint. Barbet was intrigued by the clues in the image. He noted that the nail wounds were located in the wrists of the man in the shroud. Most traditional paintings of the crucifixion depicted Jesus with the nails driven through his palms. This was curious. Barbet got permission to experiment with dead bodies. When he nailed a body to a cross by its hands, he discovered that the weight of the body simply caused the corpse to fall from the cross. The hands could not support the weight. But when Barbet drove the nails through the wrists of a dead body, it was easily supported. And he learned one other strange fact from these experiments. When the nail pierced the wrist, it damaged the median nerve, which caused the thumb to retract into the palm – and the man in the shroud had retracted thumbs.

But the Shroud of Turin yielded its most astounding secrets in the 1970s, when two top European scientists were allowed to have a go at dating the cloth. They weren't permitted to use the Carbon 14 dating method, because that would have involved destroying a piece of the shroud in the process, so Professor Max Frei, a Swiss forensic scientist, and Professor Gilbert Raes, a Belgian authority on fabric, were forced to use their pooled deductive skills to throw some light on the shroud's age and origin.

Frei recovered 48 different samples of pollen from the cloth. Pollen grains last indefinitely, and are one of the most helpful indicators of an object's age in forensic science. Most of the grains were from France and Northern Italy, which was to be expected – but seven pollen grains were from halophylic plants usually found in the Dead Sea region and other parts of Palestine. Gilbert Raes, meanwhile, had determined that the threads in the shroud derived from Middle-Eastern cotton plants. He also discovered that the threads – which were woven into a herring-bone twill weave – had been bleached before weaving. This was an extremely archaic habit.

All the new evidence seemed to signify that the shroud was authentic, and in 1974, another important discovery came to light. John Jackson and Eric Jumper, two US Air Force scientists, placed pictures of the shroud under a VP18 image analyser – a complex computerised device designed to generate three-dimensional images from two-dimensional photographs of the moon's surface.

The results were breathtaking. When viewed under the VP18 scanner, the face of the figure in the shroud literally popped up off the cloth. It was the face of a bearded man who looked remarkably like the traditional pictures of Jesus. The find unearthed a new mystery – how could a two-dimensional image contain so much three-dimensional information? This question was never answered satisfactorily.

Finally, in the 1980s, scientists were given permission to cut samples from the shroud to solve the mystery once and for all. In October 1988, these scientists announced that the Shroud of Turin could not be the burial cloth of Christ, because three independent carbon-dating tests had proved that the shroud's linen was made from flax cut between AD 1260 and 1390.

Many believers in the shroud were devastated, and some naturally questioned the reliability of the dating method employed by the scientific investigators. But the radiocarbon dating test of the shroud was impeccable in its execution. Minute pieces of the linen were delivered to laboratories in Arizona, Zurich and Oxford, along with control samples of linen that were known to belong to the Middle Ages, and to ensure that the tests were carried out without any bias, only the co-ordinator of the experiment knew which samples were genuine.

Although the results of the dating test proved that the shroud did not originate from the first century, there are still many unanswered questions. If the image on the shroud is not a depiction of Jesus, who does it represent? And if it is a fake, by what process was the image applied to the cloth? Scientists are still at loggerheads over the procedure that a thirteenth-century artist could have employed to create the shroud's realistic representation of a man who has undergone crucifixion. Even under the electron microscope there are no definite traces of the hypothetical artist's brushstrokes. Furthermore, the argument that the shroud is a mediaeval forgery fails to explain why the image on the cloth shows a man who had nails hammered through his wrists. All other mediaeval painters believed (wrongly) that Christ was nailed through the palms. How did the shroud-forger know the truth? How did he know that Christ did not wear a crown, but a cap of thorns – as depicted in the shroud? Consider, also that the man in the shroud is naked, and it was considered blasphemous to depict Christ in such a way in mediaeval times.

Here are three logical possibilities. Firstly that the scientists are not telling us the truth, perhaps because they have proved that the shroud is genuine, and therefore must admit that Jesus did exist and that he was a very unusual man. Perhaps fearing the ideological controversy that would ensue, they chose to discredit their own findings. The second possibility is that the shroud depicts a person who is not Christ, but some extraordinary man (perhaps a follower of Jesus) who was crucified between 1260 and 1390. This theory is unlikely, as no nation in the Middle East used crucifixion as an execution method during that period.

The remaining possibility is that the shroud was created by an artistic genius with a detailed knowledge of antiquity. Which artist in the late thirteenth to early fourteenth century fits the bill? The great 'Renaissance Man', Leonardo Da Vinci, was not born until 1452, and the first sighting of the shroud occurred at Constantinople in 1203, some 249 years before his birth. Yet this first mention of the shroud by military chronicler, Robert de Clari, does not tally with the time window given by the scientists. De Clari says he saw the 'sydoine' (shroud) bearing 'the figure of our Lord' during the sacking of Constantinople by the Christian knights of the Fourth Crusade. According to de Clari, the shroud was snatched by someone during the turmoil and never seen again. But this first historical mention of the cloth suggests that the estimated date of the shroud's manufacture by the scientists who carbon-dated it is erroneous. They are at least 57 years out. And the description de Clari gives of the shroud in Constantinople compares well with the shroud in Turin.

Another sinister aspect of the shroud is that the image suggests that blood was still flowing after the body was wrapped in it. Some think it suggests that Jesus was not dead when he was taken from the cross. There have also been hypothetical discussions recently among genetic engineers who think it may be possible to tackle the shroud mystery by analysing the genetic information that may be found in microscopic samples scraped from the holy cloth's bloodstains. This sampling could possibly provide a genetic profile of the man on the shroud that would give his ethnic origin, eye colour, and many more physical characteristics. A yet more controversial possibility would be the cloning of the shroud man, using a genetic technology similar to the one depicted in the sci-fi film *Jurassic Park*. It could happen in the not-too-distant future.

DID JOAN OF ARC ESCAPE THE FLAMES?

Joan of Arc was born in the picturesque village of Domremy in 1412. She was not really French, as Domremy was in those times an independent duchy of Bar, in Lorraine – which did not join the Kingdom of France until 1776. Joan did not even regard herself as a Frenchwoman, yet today the 'Maid of Orleans' as she later became known, remains France's most celebrated heroine.

Joan was one of five children. She had three brothers and a sister who died at an early age. Joan's name was not d'Arc, as some official sources still state, but Tarc – the former version of the name arose from a misspelling made by a sixteenth-century poet. Jacques Tarc, Joan's father, was Domremy's leading citizen and prosperous enough to be a co-renter of a large chateau, as well as the keeper of the local cattle pound. Most accounts of Joan's life repeat the fallacy of the hard-working peasant girl, but although Joan was not over-cossetted, her parents looked after her well and she led something of a sheltered life. Her mother, Isabelle, was very religious and taught Joan her prayers and encouraged her attempts at embroidery.

As young Joan stitched away at her needlework, the Hundred Years' War between England and France, which began in 1337, was still raging. The conflict originated in English claims to the French crown during the reign of Edward III, and war finally broke out when Philip VI of France confiscated Gascony from Edward, who retaliated by siding with the Flemish rebels against Count Louis (a French ally) and by invading northern France. After Edward's archers and men-at-arms destroyed the French fleet at the battle of Sluys in June 1340, the King of England and his eldest son, the Black Prince, were attacked by the French army as they led their forces into Ponthieu. Although they were greatly outnumbered, the English were victorious because of their superior tactical expertise and the deployment of skilled archers who used the Welsh longbow – a much-feared weapon that was lighter and more accurate than the traditional crossbow.

Edward went on to take Calais, and a seven-year truce followed. The next phase of the war commenced with English raids in northern France,

– Languedoc and Normandy. A decisive victory was won by the Black Prince at Poitiers, but Edward did not follow up his advantage. Intermittent fighting ensued, and resulted in 20 years of an uneasy peace, punctuated by short battles. Then, in 1415, Henry V renewed the English claim to the French crown. In his first martial undertaking, Henry seized the strategically important town of Harfleur, and in the following month he revived England's military prestige when his army of 5,700 fought 25,000 French soldiers at Agincourt. The latter were undisciplined, and Henry's bowmen killed 8,000 of them. The English only lost around 400.

By 1419 the English had conquered Normandy, and the Treaty of Troyes in May 1420, arranging Henry's marriage to Catherine de Valois, made him heir to the French throne. After the premature death of Henry, in 1422, the English made further conquests, and the French people needed a saviour. They were to get one in the form of a softly-spoken teenage girl.

At the age of 13, Joan Tarc was in her father's garden when she heard a strange disembodied voice coming from somewhere above her in the air, close by the local church. She heard the voice three times, and told her parents it had been that of St Michael, the Archangel. According to the teenager, the first time she had heard the voice of the Archangel, he had simply said, "Be a good girl and God will help you".

Joan's parents were naturally concerned about their daughter's far-fetched story, and nervously dismissed the tale as the invention of a lonely adolescent. But Joan continued to hear the supernatural voices, and later told her mother and father that the beings who were communicating with her had now started to reveal themselves by materialising in the form of crowned heads. Joan claimed that she had recently touched the beings, and savoured their sweet scent and had even made a vow of chastity to St Michael. Then came the astounding message from the Archangel: "You will come to the aid of the King of France."

Joan was baffled and upset by the angel's prediction, but she listened carefully to the unearthly visitant's other commands. St Michael told her that she must go into France to the fortress town of Vaucouleurs. There she would find Robert de Baudricourt, the captain of that place, and he would give her the people who would follow her.

"But I do not even know how to ride a horse, never mind make war," Joan replied, yet over the rest of the week she felt a growing urge to carry out the angel's commands.

She finally decided that she must go to Vaucouleurs, despite her father's dire warning that if she went to France, he would drown her with his own hands.

Joan mounted a horse, and to her surprise, managed to ride off for Vaucouleurs with little difficulty. When she arrived at the town, Robert de Baudricourt would not have anything to do with her, but Joan refused to leave, and finally persuaded him that it would benefit the French nation if he would send her to the Dauphin (Charles VII) at Chinon. Baudricourt relented, and sent her to Charles, who she quickly convinced of her divine mission.

Joan underwent an incredible transformation, literally overnight. She cropped her hair, dressed in male attire and suddenly became a skilled horsewoman – a knight of France. Joan led the troops to Orleans, and on 8 May 1429, after four days of intense battle, relieved the town. The English panicked and withdrew, and Joan rode into Orleans in triumph. More victories followed at Jargeau, Beaugency and Patay (where the English army were routed), and Troyes.

On 17 July of that fateful year, which proved to be a turning point in the Hundred Years' War, the Dauphin was crowned and consecrated in Reims Cathedral. Joan Tarc stood beside Charles throughout the ceremony with her battle standard in her hand, dressed in a green tunic and a rich mantle of red and gold. When the anointed king later rode in procession around the city, accompanied by Joan, thousands flocked to see him, and many who lined the procession route bowed at the teenage girl and touched her feet. She had done so much at such a young age, but dark days lay ahead.

In May 1430, she made an attempt to relieve John of Luxembourg's siege of Compiègne, but was captured after being knocked from her horse. She was imprisoned at Beaurevoir and then at Rouen, where she was put on trial in March 1431. Accused of heresy and witchcraft, Joan stood before Pierre Cauchon, the bishop of Beauvais, and Jean Le Maistre, the vice-inquisitor of France. After being found guilty, Joan was taken to a local cemetery, where a scaffold had been constructed, but she was not burned. Instead, she was forced to give a full confession and abjuration of her heresies, and the seriously ill and confused girl, thinking she was about to meet her death, confessed to worshipping evil spirits and invoking them. The guards then took her from the scaffold and put her back in a prison cell.

On 30 May 1431, the 19-year-old girl received confession before she was escorted to the market place in Rouen and declared a 'relapsed excommunicate and heretic'. She was tied to a stake nailed to a high platform, and the faggots of wood beneath it were set alight. Joan was cremated alive before a crowd of ten thousand. When the executioner later prodded about in the ashes, he shuddered when he found Joan's heart, completely intact.

And that, according to the history books, is where the story of Joan of Arc ends. But in May 1436, exactly five years after Joan was burnt as a heretic, a young woman who bore an incredible likeness to the Maid of Orleans turned up in the French town of Metz. What's more, this damsel claimed that she was Joan, but the first citizens who met the young woman called her an impostor. When Joan Tarc's two younger brothers, Petit-Jean and Pierre heard of the woman who was impersonating their deceased sister, they rode off at once to track her down. At the village of La-Grange-aux-Ormes, two miles south of Metz, they watched in amazement as a knight in full armour rode across a field where a tournament was being held, expertly pulling stakes out of the ground. The brothers galloped up to the knight and Petit-Jean said, "Who are you?"

The knight raised her visor and the two brothers recoiled as they saw that it was Joan Tarc. Petit-Jean and Pierre were struck dumb at the sight of their sister, and they suddenly noticed that most of the people at the tournament were soldiers who had served under Joan. The king's chamberlain, Nicole Lowe, was present, as was John of Metz, one of the maid's most loyal supporters. But how was this so? Joan had surely perished in the flames at Rouen. The returned martyr gave no explanation, but simply smiled enigmatically at her brothers.

Later, she accompanied them on a journey to Vaucouleurs, where she stayed for a week and went to see Robert de Baudricourt, who was naturally shocked at the sight of the girl who was supposed to have been burnt alive five years before. He took a close look at her face and trembled.

Around this time, Petit-Jean went to visit the king and told him that his sister was still alive. The king didn't seem too surprised, and instead of summoning Joan to his court, ordered his treasurer to pay Petit-Jean one hundred francs. According to the nineteenth-century historian Jules Quicherat, in his five-volume *Trial and Rehabilitation of Joan of Arc* (1841), the treasury accounts of Orleans for 9 August 1436 record that the council paid a courier who had brought letters from Joan the Maid. Quicherat also reveals that Joan's doppelganger met the king at Paris in 1440. Shortly before her arrival at his court, the king asked one of his men to impersonate him, but when Joan turned up, she was not taken in by the ruse, and demanded to see the real monarch. When the real king came out of hiding, Joan knelt at his feet, and the king said, "You are welcomed back in the name of God."

But Quicherat states that after the king and Joan had talked at length in private, the monarch suddenly declared that she was an impostor, although he never explained just how he had come to this conclusion. The woman who was identified as being Joan Tarc by Petit-Jean and Pierre Tarc, and the many soldiers who served under the Maid of Orleans, soon left Paris and was never heard from again. Was she really Joan of Arc? and if so, how did she escape the flames? To this day, no one has been able to answer these tantalising questions.

The A38 Hitch-Hiker

During the early hours of a rainy autumn morning in 1958, Harry Unsworth, a long-distance truck-driver, was driving his vehicle along the A38 towards a depot in Cullompton in Devon, when he noticed the silhouette of a man about 300 yards in front of him, standing in the middle of the road.

Unsworth slowed down and stared beyond his busy windshield wipers at the figure up ahead. He was middle-aged, with a mop of curly grey hair, and he wore a saturated grey raincoat. The man produced a torch from his pocket and flashed it straight at Unsworth, who responded by braking hard and pulling up his truck. Unsworth wound his side window down to get a better look at the hitch-hiker.

The man just stood there on the road, looking up at the driver in his cab with a dripping, expressionless face.

"Come on then!" Unsworth shouted impatiently. "Get in if you're going to!"

The man then slowly climbed into the driver's cab, and in a well-spoken voice asked Unsworth to drop him off four miles down the road at the old bridge at Holcombe. As they drove on into the night down the deserted road, the hitch-hiker suddenly started chuckling to himself. Unsworth glanced at him to try and find out what he was laughing at, but the stranger turned his face away and looked out of the passenger window, still sniggering to himself for no apparent reason. Unsworth asked him what was so funny, and the man suddenly turned towards him, his face contorted into an eerie smile.

"Did you know there was a real tragic pile-up here a few years ago?" he asked. "Arms and legs everywhere, and blood all over the road – horrible!"

He continued to recount grisly stories about all the traffic accidents that he'd witnessed on that stretch of road. Unsworth had seen a few disturbing automobile crashes himself in his time, but the hitch-hiker's gruesome blow-by-blow accounts of the injuries and fatalities really turned his stomach. He eventually told him to shut up, and was only too glad to be rid of his morbid passenger when the truck reached the agreed drop-off point at the old bridge.

Three days later, Mr Unsworth was driving his truck through the dead of night along the same section of the A38, when he came across the same hitch-hiker once again. As before, he stood right in the middle of the road, flashing a torch and waving his arm.

With a sickening sense of déjà vu, and a deep sense of foreboding, Unsworth pulled up beside the man, who again asked to be dropped off at the old bridge at Holcombe. This time the man said nothing throughout the journey, but kept smiling to himself and looking at Unsworth out of the corner of his eye. His sneaky behaviour made the truck-driver's flesh creep. When the man got out at the bridge, he didn't offer a word of thanks and walked away into the darkness.

A month after that, Unsworth was again heading along the A38 to the truck depot when he saw the dreaded hitch-hiker again, standing in the same stretch of road as before. Even the weather was the same as it had been on the two previous occasions: torrential rain. And the hitch-hiker's request? To be dropped off four miles down the road at the old bridge.

Understandably, Unsworth was decidedly reluctant to give the man a lift, but decided to take him to the confounded bridge for one last time. This time, the hitch-hiker remained silent during most of the journey, but occasionally burst out laughing.

On the following night, Harry Unsworth was again on the same route to the depot. As his vehicle neared the section of the A38 where the oddball had a habit of appearing, he anxiously scanned the road ahead. But on this occasion, the hitch-hiker was nowhere to be seen.

There was then a gap of three months before Unsworth found himself driving along the A38 again. He was whistling in his cab as he approached the place where he had first set eyes upon the hitch-hiker. He remembers smiling to himself as he thought about the crazy man with the torch. He also remembers the sight that wiped the smile off his face. Standing in the pouring rain in the middle of the road was the grey-haired man, waving his torch frantically.

Unsworth stopped next to the lunatic and wound down his window, and was astonished to hear the same hackneyed request. At this point Unsworth was more intrigued than scared, and he dropped off the man at the bridge again – but this time the hitch-hiker broke the repetitive pattern by asking him to wait whilst he went to "collect some suitcases", because he wanted to go to a destination further down the road this time.

The best part of 20 minutes elapsed and the man still hadn't returned to the truck, and as Unsworth was running to a tight schedule he couldn't afford to wait any longer. So he started up the vehicle and drove on.

Three miles down the road, Unsworth's heart jumped when he saw the hitch-hiker waving his torch in the middle of the road again. He was baffled as to how the man could possibly have travelled such a distance in so short a time. He obviously hadn't hitched a lift, for no vehicles had passed along the deserted road, and this realisation gave Unsworth the creeps. He tried to steer around the sinister figure, but as he did so, the hitch-hiker dived head-first into the path of his truck!

Unsworth slammed on the brakes and almost jack-knifed his vehicle. He leapt out of his cab expecting to find a flattened corpse, but there was nothing there. Forty feet away stood the hitch-hiker, swearing at the lorry-driver. He started to jump up and down with derision and waved his first at Unsworth. And then – he simply melted back into the night!

Unsworth ran back to his vehicle and drove off at high speed. He never encountered the A38 apparition again, but the solid-looking ghost continues to appear to other unfortunate motorists.

In December 1991, a woman driving to Taunton on the A38 was rounding a bend near the village of Rumwell, when she saw a man in a grey raincoat flashing a torch at her in the middle of the road. She couldn't brake in time and was forced to swerve her vehicle into a ditch. She was fuming as she got out of her car, ready to give the suicidal jaywalker a piece of her mind, but was amazed to find that the road was completely deserted in both directions. The man with the torch had mysteriously disappeared.

Psychical researchers who have investigated the case have concluded that the A38 hitch-hiker is probably the earth-bound spirit of one of the numerous people who have perished in car accidents on that dangerous stretch of road over the years.

THE BOY FROM NOWHERE

In the secluded fairytale state of Bavaria on the Whit Monday morning of 26 May 1828, a youth of about 17 years of age came hobbling down the almost deserted cobblestoned streets of Nuremberg. A cobbler named George Weichmann watched the young stranger, who was dressed in tattered clothes and was walking with a stiff-legged lurch through Unschlitt Square. The teenager made a pathetic moaning sound as he limped by, and the shoemaker, suspecting that he was ill, approached and offered him help. The boy seemed very confused, and mumbled something unintelligible before holding out a letter to Weichmann. The letter was addressed to 'The Captain of the 4th Squadron, 6th Cavalry Regiment, in Nuremberg'.

The cobbler was so intrigued by the bedraggled boy and his letter that he took time out to locate the captain of the 4th Squadron. He made enquiries at the New Gate guardroom, and was given the captain's address by an official. When Weichmann called at the military man's house, a servant said that his master was not home, but admitted the cobbler and the scruffily-dressed boy and offered them refreshments. The servant and the cobbler watched spellbound as the youth attacked a loaf of bread, devouring it like a wild animal. He also guzzled down a pitcher of water, but for some reason shied away from the ham and beer on the table. A candle which illuminated the gloomy side of the room soon caught the waif's attention. He walked over to it, mesmerised, and attempted to pick up the flame, and let out a scream when he burned his fingers.

The cobbler and the servant repeatedly quizzed the boy, but his only answer to every question was "Weiss nicht" (Don't know).

The other servants of the captain's household came down to look at the strange boy. They watched with amusement as he trembled in fear upon seeing the swinging pendulum of the old grandfather clock. He backed away from the timepiece in trepidation, seeming to regard it as if it were alive.

When Captain Wessenig finally arrived home, he found his servants standing in a circle around the boy, and asked what all the commotion was about. When he was told, he asked to see the letter that he carried. Its contents were two, badly-spelled, clumsily-phrased notes, fastened together. The first note read:

Honoured Captain,

I send you a lad who wishes to serve his king in the Army. He was brought to me on October 7th, 1812. I am but a poor labourer with children of my own to rear. His mother asked me to bring up the boy, and so I thought I would rear him as my own son. Since then, I have never let him go one step outside the house, so no one knows where he was reared. He, himself, does not know the name of the place, or where it is.

You may question him, Honoured Captain, but he will not be able to tell you where I live. I brought him out at night. He cannot find his way back. He has not a penny, for I have nothing myself. If you will not keep him, you must strike him dead or hang him.

The second note was dated October 1812, and ran:

This child has been baptised. His name is Kaspar; you must give him his second name yourself. I ask you to take care of him. His father was a cavalry soldier. When he is seventeen, take him to Nuremberg, to the Sixth Cavalry Regiment; his father belonged to it. I beg you to keep him until he is seventeen. He was born on April 30th, 1812. I am a poor girl; I can't take care of him. His father is dead.

As Wessenig perused the letters, the boy suddenly perked up and smiled at the captain. He then shouted out two intriguing sentences: "I want to be a soldier like my father!" and "Horse! Horse!"

Captain Wessenig was baffled by the letters, and dismissed the young ragamuffin as "either a primitive savage, or an imbecile". He had the boy taken to the police station, where what seemed to be a breakthrough occurred when the foundling was given a pencil and a sheet of paper. The policeman told the boy to write his name, and he obediently scrawled two legible words in upper case that read: 'Kaspar Hauser'. Further prodding from the policeman to continue, merely prompted the boy to say, "Don't know".

Police Sergeant Wust recorded a detailed description of the boy in a notebook. According to Wust, Kaspar Hauser was a sturdy, broad-shouldered lad of around 17 or 18 years, with a healthy complexion, light-brown hair, blue eyes, and rather small hands and feet. His clumsy gait was caused by the cluster of blisters on the soles of his unusually tender feet, presumably caused by walking a long distance. His worn-out clothes didn't seem to belong to him – the old hat, baggy trousers and badly-torn shirt were much too large, and his boots, which were reinforced with horseshoes, were too tight. The boy's toes – which protruded from them – were caked in clotted blood.

Sergeant Wust's search of the boy's clothes resulted in some curious finds. In the trouser pockets he found a packet of salt, a rosary, and two printed religious tracts, none of which provided the faintest clue to the abandoned lad's identity.

Not knowing what to do next, the police lodged Hauser in a cell. The jailer who watched him all night told Wust, "He can sit for hours without moving a limb. He does not pace the floor, nor does he try to sleep. He sits rigidly without growing in the least uncomfortable. Also, he prefers darkness to light, and can move about in it like a cat."

A physician who later examined the boy claimed that the youth's ability to sit motionless for hours was due to a distortion of his knee joints, caused by lengthy periods spent sitting with his legs straight in front of him when young, and this would account for the shaky gait he exhibited when he walked. The doctor also said that the youth was neither insane nor dull-witted, but had apparently been forcibly prevented in the most disastrous way from attaining any personal or social development.

The doctor's inspection of Hauser also confirmed that the boy could see in the dark better than in daylight, and revealed that his senses of hearing and smell were outstanding. The boy could identify animals by their scent alone, and distinguish trees by the scent of their leaves.

As the story of the mysterious teenager spread, hundreds of curious Nurembergers gathered outside Hauser's cell. They scrambled for a view through the barred window to see the oddity eat, drink, sleep and defecate.

As the weeks went by, Hauser's vocabulary seemed to expand steadily, and he was soon able to offer a fairly detailed account of his past life. This account was printed and circulated around the city as a pamphlet entitled, *Bulletin Number One – concerning the Child of Nuremberg*. The leaflet, which was signed by Burgomaster Binder of Nuremberg, stated:

He neither knows who he is, nor where he came from, for it was only at Nuremberg that he came into the world. He always lived in a hole, where he sat on straw on the ground; he never heard a sound, nor saw a vivid light. He awoke and slept and awoke again; when he awoke he found a loaf of bread and a pitcher of water beside him. Sometimes the water tasted nasty, and then he

fell asleep again, and when he woke up he found a clean shirt on; he never saw the face of the man who came to him. He had two wooden horses and some ribbons to play with; he was never ill, never unhappy in his hole, because he simply didn't know of any other type of existence ...
One day the man came into his room and put a table over his feet; something white lay on the table, and on this the man made black marks with a pencil which he put in Kaspar's fingers. This the man did several times, and when he was gone, Kaspar imitated what he had done. At last he taught him to stand and to walk, and finally carried him out of his hole. Of what happened next Kaspar has no very clear idea, until he found himself in Nuremberg with a letter in his hand.

The pamphlet turned Hauser into a celebrity overnight. He was talked about all over Europe. Who was he? Where was he from? were the questions on everybody's lips. The town press of Nuremberg printed thousands of handbills bearing Hauser's image, each carrying an appeal that read,

Anyone possessing knowledge of his true identity, or any intelligence pertaining to the same, should immediately come forward to inform the authorities and collect a cash reward.

As the handbills were being distributed, police agents were making a thorough search throughout Bavaria for the place were Hauser had been imprisoned. But no one ever came forward to collect the reward on offer, and the drawn-out police search ultimately proved futile. Anselm Ritter von Feuerbach, an eminent jurist and criminologist from Germany, visited Hauser and interrogated him for hours, and concluded that the boy's account of his early life up to his arrival in Nuremberg was genuine. The renowned lawyer also hinted that he had solved the Hauser enigma and intimated that it involved an epic scandal, but he refused to go into more detail and quickly left the city.

Rumours abounded naming Kaspar Hauser as the illegitimate son of almost every aristocratic rake of Europe. The theory went that Hauser had been kept hidden away by his high-born parent for 16 years before finally being turned loose when it was judged that time had eradicated the danger of a scandal.

Professor George Friedrich Daumer, a distinguished educationalist and philosopher, was appointed to be Hauser's guardian. Daumer was fascinated by the boy's incredible naivety. He watched an amused Hauser look behind a mirror after glancing into it, and on another occasion saw him stroke a ball that had bounced into his lap, as if he regarded it as an animate being. Daumer also discovered that Hauser was ambidextrous and had some artistic talent. This artistic faculty was soon developed under Daumer's guidance, and within a matter of months, Hauser was executing exquisite pencil drawings of still life and rural scenes.

In the summer of 1829, Professor Daumer helped his protégé write his autobiography. In the August of that year the book was published, but it proved to be something of an anti-climax, for the autobiographical work threw no new light on the Hauser mystery. It looked as if the people of Nuremberg were losing interest in their lionised citizen, but their interest was rekindled in a most dramatic way when reports circulated of an attack on Hauser.

On the afternoon of 7 October 1829, the teenager was found prostrate in Professor Daumer's cellar. He was unconscious, his shirt was torn to the waist, and he was bleeding from a gash in his forehead. He was carried upstairs and put to bed, where he gradually regained consciousness and Daumer was able to ask him to give an account of what had happened. Hauser said that he had been attacked by a tall, sinister-looking assailant wearing a top hat, black silken mask, dark clothes, and black leather gloves. The masked man had struck Hauser once with a heavy cosh, and then fled.

What was the motive behind the attack? This was just another unanswered question of the Hauser enigma. When several people came forward saying they had seen a suspicious-looking character leaving Daumer's house, the police combed the area, but the attacker was never found. The authorities now believed that Hauser was in danger, and moved him from Daumer's house to the home of a certain Freiherr von Tucher. The jurist Anselm Ritter von Feuerbach was summoned to become his new guardian. Two police constables were also assigned to be Hauser's bodyguards, and they both slept in the same room as him.

In May 1833, von Feuerbach suffered a paralytic stroke and died. He had been compiling a detailed report on his ward, and many thought the chronicle would finally reveal the answers to the Hauser mystery. The report, entitled *Example of a Crime Against the Life of the Soul of a Man*, stated that Hauser was a legitimate child, because no one would go to such lengths to hide a bastard offspring. Therefore, von Feuerbach speculated, Kaspar Hauser had to be in line of succession to a very high position – a position exalted enough to facilitate Hauser's removal and cruel confinement. Since Hauser's confinement was voluntarily brought to an end after a certain period of time, it followed that some other person had taken over the position formerly usurped from Hauser. And according to von Feuerbach, the only position that was exalted enough to justify such clandestine manipulations was a royal one.

After his controversial conclusion, von Feuerbach left the pages blank, because as a lawyer he knew he would be libelling the crown (a most serious offence in the nineteenth century) if he so much as pointed the finger of suspicion at any particular royal family member. Von Feuerbach's thesis was translated into most European languages, and was followed by rumours claiming that von Feuerbach had not died from a stroke at all, but had been poisoned by people in high places who thought the German criminologist was getting too close to the truth.

Curiously, the eccentric English aristocrat Lord Stanhope suddenly took an interest in the Hauser case. He visited Germany and convinced the Nuremberg Council to give him permission to lodge the teenager in the town of Ansbach, some 25 miles away from Hauser's then residence. A friend of Lord Stanhope, Dr Meyer, was appointed as Hauser's tutor, and Captain Hickel, a military officer, was given the task of protecting the boy. Hickel must have been somewhat embarrassed when, on the afternoon of 11 December 1833, the boy he was supposed to be shielding from harm came staggering through the doorway with a deep knife-wound in his abdomen. Hauser had gone out earlier that day to enjoy a walk through the deserted, snow-covered Hofgarten, Ansbach's public park.

"Man ... stabbed!" gasped the mortally wounded Hauser. "Knife! Hofgarten ... gave purse ... Go look ... quickly!"

Dr Meyer and his wife came running to the teenager's aid, and Captain Hickel raced to Hofgarten, hoping for a confrontation with the assailant. Hickel only saw Hauser's set of footprints as he trudged through the snow in the park, but he found the silk purse Hauser had mentioned. He picked it up and opened it. It contained a baffling note written backwards in mirror writing:

Hauser will be able to tell you how I look, whence I came from, and who I am. To spare him that task, I will tell you myself. I am from ... On the Bavarian border ... On the River ... My name is "M.L.O."

But contrary to the note's claims, Hauser did not know who the man was, or where he was from. But from his deathbed he managed to tell an interesting story about that fateful day. He said he had gone to the park to meet a man who had contacted him earlier by sending a message through a labourer. The man, who was described as tall, with dark whiskers and wearing a black cloak, approached him in the park with the question, "Are you Kaspar Hauser?" When Hauser nodded, the stranger handed him a silk purse. As Hauser opened it, the man suddenly stabbed him before running off. Kaspar dropped the purse and stumbled homeward through the snow.

A massive manhunt quickly got underway, but the tall, dark-whiskered man was never caught, and some wondered if he had ever existed, for he left no tracks at the scene of the crime.

Until Kaspar Hauser slipped into a coma on the afternoon of 17 December, Dr Meyer continually asked him if he had inflicted the wound himself to get attention, and Hauser's persistent answer had been a shake of his head. Later that day, minutes before Hauser passed away, he was heard to say, "I didn't do it myself".

The post-mortem, performed by three doctors, revealed that a sharp instrument had come through the diaphragm just below the ribcage and had been thrust upwards until it penetrated the heart. Two of the doctors were certain that the murderer had been left-handed, and one said he was absolutely sure that Kaspar Hauser could not have stabbed himself.

Today, the debate still rages. Some think Hauser was a hoaxer who craved attention, while others think he was the victim of a conspiracy. A monument now stands marking the spot in the Ansbach park where Hauser was stabbed, and the Latin inscription upon it states:

On this place, for mysterious reasons, one mysterious figure was murdered by another mysterious figure.

Not far away from the monument, in Ansbach Cemetery, the epitaph on Hauser's gravestone reads:

Here lies the Riddle of our Time. His Birth was Unknown, his Death, Mysterious.

THE GIANT SPIDER OF THE UKRAINE

The following creepy tale has been buzzing around the Internet for years and has also appeared in various tabloid newspapers in Europe, but has never been reported in the British or American press.

In the summer of 1990, police in Russia found a resident in a block of flats in the Ukraine, lying dead on the floor of an elevator. The man had two puncture holes in the side of his neck, which was badly bruised yellow and blue. At the post-mortem, the coroner established that the man in the elevator had died through shock and loss of blood. About 1.5 litres of blood were missing from the body, yet there had been no bloodstains in the elevator. It was as if something had sucked the blood straight out of the dead man, but the Russian police couldn't accept such an outlandish explanation.

A month later, the police were called to the same block of flats because a girl of 13 was trapped in the elevator, which was stuck between the fourth and fifth floors. Residents had heard the girl screaming frantically, and when the police arrived with three members of the local fire service and gained access to the elevator her screams had stopped. They found the child lying on the floor of the elevator. She was dead, and two small puncture marks were later found on the girl's left breast, which was heavily bruised. The residents understandably refused to use the faulty elevator, and were convinced that a vampire, or some other blood sucking creature was at large in the block of flats.

Police attempted to play down the seemingly unsolvable deaths, and one former KGB propaganda minister, Leonid Keernev, suggested that the girl had probably died after injecting heroin, but the dead girl's parents threatened to sue the official, because their daughter had never taken drugs and no syringe was found in the elevator.

To try and get to the bottom of the matter, a Russian detective and a sergeant entered the lift and rode it continuously up and down. The two men were armed with pistols and carried flashlights and two-way radios.

But nothing happened until three days later, when the lift was travelling upwards and it suddenly halted between the fifth and sixth floors of the building. The lights went out, so the men switched on their torches and two-way radios to alert their colleagues, who were playing cards in a police van in the street below.

The two trapped men waited apprehensively, perhaps wondering if some ghostly vampire was about to materialise. There was complete silence for about three minutes; then they heard something scuttling about above their heads. Something was moving along the roof of the elevator. The detective noticed a black square – almost a foot across – set in the roof of the elevator, where an access panel had come away. The lift was so old that the panel had probably fallen off because of rust. He shone his torch through the square hole in the roof, and the beam from his torch lit up the lift shaft above and the steel cables supporting the lift. Something peered back through that hole that made the detective's blood turn to ice. A black, hairy head, the size of an orange, with a bunch of black, gleaming eyes, the size of grapes, peered down at him.

The sergeant was revolted by the freakish-looking animal and raised his Beretta and aimed it at the thing, but the detective calmly ordered him not to fire yet.

"What the heck is it?" said the petrified police sergeant, trembling, almost dropping his torch with nerves.

"Turn your torch off," hissed the detective.

"What? No way! I'm sorry, sir, but I'm not taking my eyes of that hideous thing," the sergeant protested, sweating heavily.

"You can tell it doesn't like light," said the detective. "You keep your torch on, then, and I'll turn mine off. Don't make any sudden moves, and tell the men downstairs to stand by."

The detective switched off his light, and watched as first one long, hairy leg and then another, slid further into the lift. Suddenly, the sergeant's nerves got the better of him, because he had three phobias: fear of the dark; fear of enclosed spaces; and arachnophobia – a fear of spiders – and that horrible thing hanging through the hole in the ceiling looked like a dirty great, overgrown spider. So the sergeant freaked out and in his panic he dropped his torch – and his nerves cost him his life. The torch hit the floor and smashed. Before the detective could switch on his torch, the enormous hairy black spider had dropped into the lift with lightning agility, and had bitten the only thing in the lift that was moving excitedly. The spider sank its giant fangs into the unfortunate sergeant's face, and hung on like a vice as it sucked out his blood.

The detective switched on his torch and watched in impotent horror as the whole nightmarish drama unfolded. The sergeant was screaming hysterically, and the spider was like some alien creature from another planet. Its body was the size of a Jack Russell dog, and its eight hairy legs were almost three feet long. The freak insect's mouthparts were still embedded into the sergeant's face, and as it drained his life-blood, the spider's body throbbed and turned a deep red.

The terrified detective forced himself to act. He took aim and shot twice at the sickening spider. The first shot missed, and the second bullet blasted one of the spider's legs off, but when the bullet ricocheted off the wall, it bounced back and smashed the torch bulb. The lift was once again plunged into absolute darkness. The sergeant suddenly stopped screaming and his body hit the floor with a dull thump, and the detective felt sick as he felt bristly hairs brushing against him as the wounded spider scrambled past and climbed back up to its lair through the hole in the elevator's roof.

When the police and firemen opened the elevator, they found the dead sergeant, whose terror-stricken face was bruised and bloody – and on the floor, in the corner, sat the traumatised detective. Nearby on the elevator floor was the long, hairy, black leg of the spider, still twitching. The detective remained speechless for a while, then blurted out the incredible story.

The Russian authorities quickly hushed up the incident, but news of the story leaked out via the Internet, and a version of the story also appeared in a Turkish newspaper, but was quickly denounced as an fabrication or at least, exaggeration.

It was claimed by some that the giant spider was a deformed black widow spider that had been mutated by the radioactive fallout from the recent Chernobyl nuclear plant disaster. Later reports on the Internet said Russian troops had destroyed the spider with a flame-thrower, and had then discovered that the insect had laid dozens of eggs in a large cocoon at the top of the lift shaft.

HOMER – MAN, WOMAN OR COMMITTEE?

The stirring tales of the *Iliad* and the *Odyssey* have been thrilling readers since they were penned by a blind Greek poet named Homer in the eighth century BC. But what do we know of Homer? Not much, according to the historians. They say that it is quite possible that the Ionian poet never existed; Homer may have been the name of a group of writers who collectively wrote the *Iliad* and the *Odyssey*, as well as the mock-heroic Greek poem, *The Battle of the Frogs* and *The Mice*, and the so-called Homeric hymns.

The *Iliad* and the *Odyssey* as we know them today are based on texts that were edited in the sixth century BC. The Athenians tampered with a considerable proportion of the *Iliad* text to increase their role in it, and in the second century BC, two scholars – Aristarchus of Samothrace and Aristophanes of Byzantium – meddled with the wording of the *Iliad* in Alexandria. The extant texts are substantially those of Aristarchus.

So much for the classical texts, but what information do we have on the man who is supposed to have authored them? The Greek historian Herodotus (c485-425 BC) tells us that Homer's mother, Critheis, an impoverished orphan, lived in Smyrna, Asia Minor. After becoming pregnant out of wedlock, she left Asia Minor and settled at a place near the River Meles in Greece, where she gave birth to a son whom she named Melesigenes (after the river). Melesigenes was known in his later years by the nickname of 'Homer' – which means 'blind man' in Greek. Critheis later returned to Smyrna and secured employment as a housekeeper to a music and literature teacher named Phemius, whom she later married. Phemius took to his stepson as if he were of his own flesh and blood, and tutored him daily in music and the written word. As a result, young Homer excelled at school and upon the death of his stepfather was appointed to run it, soon gaining the status of a local celebrity.

He later became friends with a wealthy traveller from Leukas named Mentes and accompanied him on a tour of Italy, but upon reaching Ithaca, he caught an eye infection that worsened until he was almost blind. Mentes reluctantly left his friend in the care of a doctor called Mentor, and continued on his journey. Mentor had a vast knowledge of the legendary exploits of Odysseus and the Trojan War, and Homer, being a good listener, took in every detail of the doctor's tales. When the Odyssey was written many years later, Homer immortalised Mentor by naming the teacher of Odysseus's son after him.

Mentor could not find a remedy for Homer's eye infection, and Homer decided to make an attempt to return home before his predicament worsened, but he had only got as far as Colophon, in Asia Minor, when he became totally blind. He was taken back to Smyrna, where he decided to dedicate himself to poetry, and having no school to provide him with any financial support, set out to live the life of a wandering poet. Homer's meanderings brought him to a place called the New Wall (Neon Teichos) where he earned a meagre living by reciting verse. He later drifted to Cumae, where he begged the town council to support him for his poetry recitals, but one waspish councillor complained that if Cumae fed every blind man who came to the city, the people would soon be overrun with vagrants.

The council decided not to fund Homer, who left and travelled from town to town for many years, until he finally settled at Chios, where he was employed to teach the children of a wealthy man. Homer became so well-liked at Chios that the inhabitants later claimed that Homer had been born among them. Tales of the blind poet's wisdom reached Greece, and when Homer visited the island of Samos, he was regarded as a sort of god-like figure, and was asked to take part in the religious festivals. He left Samos, bound for Athens, but upon reaching the island of Ios, he suddenly became seriously ill and died from what was probably a stroke.

After Homer's death, stories of the legendary poet travelled throughout Greece, Italy and Spain, and the bards of those countries began to recite Homer's poems. The *Odyssey* and *Iliad* were suddenly held in such esteem that they were recited and re-enacted every four years at the Panathenaea festivals in Athens.

That then, is a summary of Homer's life, according to Herodotus, a historian who has been criticised for credulity and reckless interpolation, but admired for his charming narrative. Herodotus named the bird of immortality 'Phoenix' after confusing the mythical creature with 'phoinix' – the Greek name for the palm tree which the bird was said to sit upon. It is no wonder then, that many scholars have treated the Greek historian's account of Homer's life with caution; some students of history regard his version of the bard's life as an outright work of speculation based on legends and figments of his imagination.

One such notable person was the English satirist, novelist and translator, Samuel Butler (1835-1902). Butler stunned the literary world in 1897 with the publication of his book, *The Authoress of the Odyssey*, in which he defended his long-held conviction that Homer was a woman. What led the writer to this unusual conclusion? Well, Butler re-read the Odyssey, and while perusing the part of the book that describes the enchantress, Circe, he was struck by the depth of her character in comparison with the stilted, almost wooden males of the work. Butler suspected that a woman, and a young one at that, may have been the elusive author, and not the blind old man of legend. Butler read on and began to see more clues in the text, such as in the description of a rudder on the front of a ship, which suggested that the authoress had no idea of seamanship – a male skill. Homer clearly wasn't too familiar with woodwork either, because he (or she) tells us how seasoned timber was cut from a growing tree. Butler noted these errors and many more to back up his 'Homera' hypothesis, and concluded his work by identifying Princess Nausicaa, the daughter of the *Odyssey's* Queen Arete, as Homer. Butler also deduced that Nausicaa's home town was Trapani, on the west coast of Sicily, a conclusion he reached after sifting through the text of the *Odyssey* for geographical details.

Butler's book was largely ignored by the scholars of his day. Professor Benjamin Jowett, Oxford's celebrated expert on Ancient Greece unashamedly admitted that he had not even bothered to glance at Butler's book. Despite rejection from the cognoscenti, Butler managed to convince George Bernard Shaw, Robert Graves and many other writers that the person who laid the foundation stone of western literature was a woman. Although Butler's theory is entirely plausible, it has been almost totally ignored by modern scholars.

Date With Death

In October 1967, a beautiful 21-year-old woman named Christine started work as a secretary at the Life Assurance Company in London. All her workmates were dating, and were surprised that she wasn't, as she was very attractive. On her first day at work, Jack, one of her colleagues at the company, asked her if he could take her out, but Christine politely turned him down, and said she was already interested in someone else.

"Lucky rascal," Jack remarked, and he asked her who her boyfriend was. Christine blushed and shrugged but said nothing. Another secretary who had been listening to the conversation, stopped typing and asked her the same question.

"To be honest, I don't know," she said.

"Eh? How do you mean you don't know?" laughed Jack. "You must know, surely."

"I haven't actually spoken to him, but I've seen him lots of times. I can tell he likes me, the way he always smiles at me when I see him."

"Where do you see him then?" asked the junior manager, Frank. He had also been listening to the conversation while filing away a claim. He was almost 40, and Christine felt embarrassed talking to him about what must seem like an infantile crush.

"Oh, er, well, I first saw him about a month ago, as he was trying to hail a taxi in Piccadilly. He had a black suit on; he was very neat looking. And he has jet black hair and sort of ... oh, I don't know, please stop asking me!" Christine hid her face behind her hands and added, "Mind your own business, you lot."

"She's embarrassed," Frank said, and laughed. But he turned to the others and said, "All right, everyone, back to work. You lot have been watching too much Peyton Place."

On the Monday morning of the following week, an office boy came up to Christine with an envelope in his hand and asked: "Are you Christine?"

"Yes," Christine nodded.

"A nice-looking fellah came into reception and asked me to give this to you. Must be a secret admirer, eh?"

Christine smiled and started to open the envelope. Meanwhile, Frank,

Jack and the other secretary stopped work and looked at Christine, aching to know what the letter was about.

Jack couldn't stand the suspense any longer and said, "Well, come on then, what does it say?"

Christine smirked as she read the letter, then said, "It's from him."

"Who?" Frank asked.

"That man I like, remember?" Christine read out the letter in a faltering, timid voice: "Dear Christine ... our paths through life have finally met ... Please meet me at on the corner of Regent Street ... off Piccadilly ... near the taxi rank at five thirty."

The letter was signed, 'Tall, dark and handsome'.

For the remainder of that day, Christine couldn't get her feet back on the ground, and seemed to be in a blissful world of her own as she tried to concentrate on her work. Jack occasionally tried to put her off the date, warning that the admirer might be someone playing a prank, or even some kind of pervert. But when work finished, Christine headed straight for the toilet and rummaged through her handbag. She brushed her long hair and put on some foundation and lipstick. She dabbed on her perfume and left the building with the other staff. Frank wished her luck, but Jack pointed to a passing pensioner and jokingly said, "I bet you he's the fellah who wrote the letter."

Christine went window shopping in Shaftesbury Avenue to kill time – then she spotted Jack peeping at her from the corner of nearby Dean Street. She marched up to him and angrily asked what he thought he was playing at, spying on her. Jack felt ridiculous and explained that he wasn't spying, he was just concerned about her.

"I just thought I'd see you were okay, in case the man you're meeting is a lunatic. That's all," he said sheepishly.

"Yes, well, I'm quite all right thank you very much," replied Christine, and she told Jack to beat it.

The young man reluctantly did so. He was not just worried about her safety, he was secretly very upset at the secretary meeting the man of her dreams.

At precisely 5.30pm Christine's dead body was found a few feet from the arranged rendezvous point. Two shoppers who had witnessed the whole thing described how the girl had just fallen down like a rag doll, and seemed to die instantly. The post-mortem examination cited the cause of death as heart failure, although Christine had never suffered from heart trouble in her life. All her new friends at work were devastated, and Frank cried openly, because she had been such a sweet girl.

Shortly afterwards, events took an even more sinister turn when Jack went to a trendy night club in Wardour Street called the Flamingo one night, and there he met a stunningly beautiful girl called Janet. She was exceptionally attractive, and they could hardly dance because there were so many male admirers around her, trying to catch her attention. Jack bravely danced next to the girl, and later bought her a drink. They both chatted at the bar, and seemed to be getting along nicely, but suddenly Janet stopped speaking in mid-sentence and looked at someone who was standing behind Jack.

"Hello there," she said, and Jack followed her eyes to see a very tall man, aged about 30, dressed in a black sweater. Everyone else had their long hair styled like the Beatles, but the tall, dark stranger had his heavily oiled hair cropped closely to the side, like someone out of the 1950s. The man then said something to Janet which, for some reason, made Jack's blood run cold.

"Hello Janet, looks like our paths through life have finally met."

Jack had heard that line before, but couldn't quite recall where, because he'd been drinking quite heavily. But he'd definitely heard those words before and experienced a strong sense of déjà vu.

The man leaned forward and kissed Janet, and the girl, who had struck Jack as a rather brazen type, seemed to melt and become dewy-eyed in the stranger's presence. The tall man shouldered Jack aside and started to chat to Janet. Disgruntled, Jack went to the toilet, and when he returned, he was pleased to see that the man was gone. Janet stood at the bar, seemingly oblivious to the three men clustered round her asking if they could get her a drink.

Jack walked up to her and tugged her arm.

"Where's that man gone?" he said.

"Oh! He's left …" Janet said, and she sighed and added, "He's lovely … I just wanted him to take me home."

"I thought he was weird. What was his name?"

Janet just shrugged.

"I'm meeting him tomorrow. I can't wait. He's really sophisticated. Not like this lot in here."

"Eh? Where are you meeting him?"

Janet's face seemed to light up with joy and she said: "On the corner of

Regent Street near Piccadilly Circus. He's got a really sexy voice ... and a way with words ... real manly he is. Oh! he'll certainly do me."

A broad, muscular bouncer turned up, told Jack to move out of the way and playfully slapped Janet on her bottom. He then put his arm around her and listened attentively while she again related her tale of the intellectual, handsome stranger and her forthcoming date with him. The bouncer didn't seem too pleased and tried to persuade her to go on a date with him the next day instead. Janet just laughed and told him that he had no chance of competing with the tall, dark man.

On the following evening, shortly before eight o'clock, Jack turned up near Janet's rendezvous point on Regent Street, burning with curiosity and a strange sense of dread. He suddenly experienced a strong feeling of déjà vu, and into his mind leapt the line in Christine's letter from the anonymous admirer. The line which had read: 'Our paths through life have finally met.' That had been the same line uttered by the man in the black suit at the Flamingo last night. But surely it could be nothing more than a weird coincidence?

As Jack loitered about, he noticed the bouncer from the Flamingo approaching briskly from the opposite direction, but the burly man hadn't noticed him yet. Meanwhile, a large crowd of people was gathering near the cab rank further down the street. Jack had assumed the people were queuing for taxis, but they weren't. As he drew near he realised that the crowd was standing around the body of a beautiful young girl in a bright dress. Someone cried out, "Call an ambulance!" and another man kneeling by the body gloomily declared that it was too late. "She's dead" he said. "Look at her eyes – wide open – and her heart's stopped beating."

When the bouncer looked at the lifeless body he opened his mouth and seemed speechless with shock. Then he cried out, "Janet! Oh no! Janet!"

It was Janet from the Flamingo, lying on the steps of the cinema, quite dead, her lovely features drained of all colour, her lovely body lifeless. Jack felt an icy chill racing through his bones when he saw her lying there, and was convinced that Janet and Christine had somehow both been courted by Death – Death in the form of a tall, handsome stranger. It was as if both girls had had a date with Death. Janet's inert body was taken into the ambulance and was rushed to hospital, but she was pronounced dead on arrival.

There is an eerie postscript to this shocking story.

Jack left the Life Assurance firm in 1971, but in 1979 he met a former work colleague from the Brian Haines Company, who told him that in 1972, another secretary from the firm had gone to meet a young man she had met in Hyde Park. The man had asked her to meet him on the corner of Regent Street, and the secretary had only been waiting five minutes at the rendezvous point when she suffered a tremendous cerebral aneurysm – a violent bursting of a blood vessel in her brain, and she fell down dead.

One of the people who witnessed the secretary's death – a cabby at the taxi rank – told how a strange tall man in a black suit stood impassively over the girl as she collapsed onto the pavement, making no attempts to revive her, or administer first aid, or even to bend down to see how she was. The stranger exhibited no concern whatsoever, but simply turned round and walked off into the night in the direction of Jermyn Street.

Many people who still recall the strange spate of fatal incidents in that part of central London are of the opinion that something more sinister than coincidence was responsible for the deaths of the three young women – who had all apparently had a date with Death.

The Brahan Seer

In the year 1600, Coinneach (Kenneth in Gaelic) Odhar was born on the Isle of Lewis in the Outer Hebrides. Odhar was a poor farm labourer until tales of his prophetic powers reached the ears of his feudal overlord, Lord Mackenzie of Kintail. Lord Mackenzie was so intrigued by the stories of the Scot's mysterious talent that he summoned Coinneach to live on his land at Brahan Castle, near the Firth of Cromarty. Shortly after Coinneach's arrival on the Brahan lands, Lord Mackenzie died, and was succeeded by one of the Earls of Seaforth.

The 'Brahan Seer', as Coinneach was known, was taken on as a resident prophet of the Seaforth family, and he lodged in a sod-roofed cottage on the Brahan estate. Some doubted his purported powers of second sight, and one such doubter, an elderly man named Duncan Macrae of Glenshiel, asked the Brahan Seer to tell him how he would end his days. Coinneach Odhar told Macrae that he would die by the sword. Many laughed at this prediction; after all, who would stoop to killing an old man with a sword?

But years later, in 1654, the English General George Monck was leading a troop of Parliamentary soldiers up towards Kintail, and a company of his men encountered old Duncan Macrae, who was walking across the hills to his home. The soldiers challenged Macrae – who was unfamiliar with the English tongue – and he panicked and reached for his broadsword. A nervous English soldier reacted to the old man's sudden movement by hacking him to death with a sword – exactly as the Brahan Seer had predicted years previously.

In 1630, the Seer was crossing a vast expanse of moorland when he suddenly stopped and soliloquised:

"Oh! Drummrossie, thy bleak moor shall, ere many generations have passed away, be stained with the best blood of the Highlands. Glad I am that I will not see the day! Heads will be lopped off by the score, and no mercy shall be shown."

The Brahan Seer was accurately describing the battle of Culloden that would be fought in the area 116 years later, when the Duke of Cumberland's Royal troops completely routed the Highlanders of the Young Pretender, and many heads were indeed lopped off. Cumberland's barbaric tactics at Culloden earned him the title of 'Butcher'.

Another of the Seer's predictions that was regarded as nonsense at the time, was his assertion that, one day, strings of black carriages, horseless and bridleless, would pass through the Highlands, drawn by a fiery chariot. That was the only language available to the seventeenth-century oracle to describe the railways, and their colossal, fire-burning steam engines, that were to come to the Highlands in the Victorian era.

The Brahan Seer also declared that ships would one day sail round the back of Tomnahurich Hill. Those who laughed at the seemingly ridiculous prophecy never lived to see the construction of Thomas Telford's Caledonian Canal, which linked the North Sea with the Irish Sea, via the Great Glen. The great canal cut a path round the back of Tomnahurich Hill, and so it came to pass that ships, or at least barges, were able to sail behind the hill – 150 years after the Brahan Seer prophesied that it would be so.

The Celtic soothsayer also foresaw three Scottish ecological disasters. The first of these has already come to pass. The Seer predicted that a Loch above Beauly would burst its banks and destroy, in its rush, a village in its vicinity.

In 1967, an unusually heavy rain storm was responsible for causing the hydro-electric dam at Torachilty to overflow, and this in turn caused the River Conlon to burst its banks. The ensuing flood destroyed buildings, cattle and crops, and created havoc for the village of Conlon Bridge, which is only five miles from Beauly.

The second, as yet unfulfilled prophecy of the Brahan Seer states that when 'Loch Shiel in Kintail shall become so narrow that a man shall leap across it, the salmon shall desert the Loch and the River Shiel.'

The third bleak prophecy concerned 'horrid black rains' that will fall on the land. Perhaps the Seer is describing a type of acid rain, or perhaps even fallout from an atomic war, or a nuclear-power plant disaster, like the one that occurred in the 1980s at Chernobyl.

In the end, the Brahan Seer sealed his own fate with one of his prophecies when he told the Countess of Seaforth that her husband had a mistress in Paris. The Seer was correct about the adulterous affair, but the Countess was so outraged by the information, that she ordered that the psychic should be boiled in tar as a warlock. A classic case of shooting the messenger.

The Seer was taken to Chanonry Point on the Moray Firth to be executed, but shortly before he was cruelly boiled alive in a barrel of molten tar he made his last prediction, which concerned the future of the Seaforth family. He said that the last of the Seaforth line would be deaf and dumb, and added that the inheritor would be a 'white-hooded lassie' who would kill her sister.

One hundred and fifty years later, in January 1815, Francis Mackenzie, the last of the line, died of a sinister illness that left him deaf and dumb, and two years afterwards, his eldest surviving daughter, Mary, who inherited his estate, was wearing the traditional white hood to mark the recent death of her husband as she drove a carriage through woods. With her was her sister Caroline, and during the journey, the ponies bolted and the carriage overturned, injuring Mary and killing Caroline. So the Brahan seer's last predictions also proved to be true.

WHO WAS THE BARD OF STRATFORD?

What do the following eminent individuals have in common? Charles Dickens, Sigmund Freud, Charles de Gaulle, Daphne du Maurier, Mark Twain, Walt Whitman, Benjamin Disraeli and Charles Chaplin.

The answer is that none of them believed that the 38 plays attributed to Shakespeare were actually written by the great bard. Freud thought that Shakespeare had nothing to justify his claims, and believed that the real author of *Hamlet* and *King Lear* was the Seventeenth Earl of Oxford, Edward de Vere.

It is somewhat ironic that Mark Twain and Charlie Chaplain held the view that Shakespeare could not have produced the plays credited to him because he was a mere country bumpkin, lacking in education. Yet Twain himself was born in a small frontier village and left school at eleven years of age, while Chaplin, who experienced an impoverished childhood after his father died, received his first taste of education at the Hanwell poor law institution!

One of the first people to doubt that Shakespeare existed at all was a Dr James Wilmot, an associate of Samuel Johnson and a fellow of Trinity College, Oxford. Wilmot researched the Bard of Stratford for four years, and in 1785 reached the conclusion that the plays of Shakespeare were penned by none other than Sir Francis Bacon. Just what led him to this conclusion will never be known, for upon Wilmot's death, his housekeeper for some reason threw the fruit of his researches onto the fire.

Anyone who has slogged their way through one of Bacon's scientific essays will scoff at Wilmot's claim, but adherents to the Bacon theory (who call themselves Baconians) assert that their candidate certainly had the educational background to produce the plays and chose the name 'Shakespeare' as a mere nom de plume. They point out that Shakespeare's works indicate that the author was a true Renaissance Man, with a vast knowledge of law, history, seamanship, medicine and the Continent – just like Bacon.

If we are to believe that the Baconians have a case, then there must have been a gigantic conspiracy in the late sixteenth century, and the conspirators would have included the rector of the Stratford church where the records of Shakespeare's birth, marriage and death are kept, along with the baptismal records of his children. Other individuals would also have been implicated in the Bacon Conspiracy: people like Ben Johnson, King James, Queen Elizabeth I, the Second Earl of Southampton, the Second Earl of Essex, and the 26 members of Shakespeare's acting troupe, the King's Men.

Far fetched? Not according to the Baconians, who cite two pieces of information to back up their argument. The first piece of 'evidence' concerns an enigmatic inscription on Shakespeare's monument in Poet's Corner at Westminster Abbey. Upon the monument's marble scroll, there is an inscribed quotation from *The Tempest*, Shakespeare's last play. The quotation has been hacked about and is laced with apparently intentional spelling mistakes, but a line in the middle of the inscription stands out, because, for some unaccountable reason, it contains only two words: 'Shall Dissolve'. Cryptologists have now discovered that if the letters of those two words are set out in the 13 squares of a well-known seventeenth-century cipher, they do indeed spell out: Francis Bacon.

Alexander Pope, who had a hand in the erection of the Shakespeare monument in 1741, was a master of cipher, and was probably behind the encoded message on the marble scroll. If so, what was he trying to say? That Bacon was Shakespeare?

Another curious fact came to light in 1989 when a producer from Yorkshire Television's documentary programme, *First Tuesday*, obtained permission to X-ray Shakespeare's grave in Stratford's Holy Trinity Church, which is visited by thousands of tourists every year. The results of the X-ray proved, beyond a shadow of a doubt, that Shakespeare's 'grave' was completely empty. Nothing was there – not even the slightest trace of the bard's bones.

In March 1994, a book called *The Shakespeare Controversy* by Graham Phillips and Martin Keatman was published. The book claimed that the most famous playwright of all time was a secret agent who used his theatrical career as a cover. In a nutshell, the authors' theory is that through his fellow playwrights, Christopher Marlowe and Anthony Munday, Shakespeare was embroiled in a network of spies, informers and saboteurs led by Sir Walter Raleigh and Sir Francis Walsingham, a puritanical Protestant and one of Queen Elizabeth's principal Secretaries of State. The authors point out that the idea of Shakespeare as an agent in the Elizabethan Secret Service is not as absurd as it first seems. So many in his circle certainly were – people like Munday, Marlowe, and Shakespeare's patron, Lord Strange, who was involved with the government network of spies. Lord Strange informed Sir William Cecil of the Hesketh Plot, a planned Catholic conspiracy to overthrow the government.

The authors of the book go on to say that William Shakespeare's sudden death in 1616 was probably the result of being poisoned by Raleigh, who had just been released from the Tower. Raleigh had been imprisoned after being accused of being a spy by a mysterious agent named William Hall – perhaps an alias for Shakespeare? So upon his release, Raleigh quickly sought out the agent who had put him behind bars and exacted his revenge.

What are we to make of all this? Are the Baconians right? Was Shakespeare a spy? And does it really matter in the end? Whoever he was, he left us with a magnificent legacy of plays and sonnets which are still performed and read all over the world. As the Bard himself wrote in *Romeo and Juliet*: 'What's in a name? That which we call a rose, by any other name would smell as sweet.'

THE ANCIENT ONES

The following very old legend is mentioned all over the world by different nations and tribes in one form or another; many mystics and students of the occult say it is the true history of mankind.

According to the legend, a long time ago, long before the flood, long before humans walked upon the Earth, intelligent, god-like beings came across our world and fought among themselves over the ownership of the planet. This ancient legend says that there was a war in the heavens over the possession of Earth, and that a brilliant scientist-like figure named Lucifer was defeated by a group of super-intelligent beings known as the Elohim.

The rebellious Lucifer and his followers took refuge beneath the planet's surface in caves and caverns, and the Elohim took possession of the Earth, which they called Eden, and all other extraterrestrial beings were warned off from the planet's vicinity. The mystics say that there are ancient texts in Tibet which tell of how the gods destroyed horrific dragons and monsters that lived in the land and the seas; could these monsters have been the dinosaurs, which were mysteriously wiped out 65 million years ago?

What became of Lucifer and his cohorts? According to the legends, they are still lying dormant beneath the earth, but their physical bodies have long since decayed, and only their evil spirits now exist. The folklore experts of the world refer to these underground spirits as the Ancient Ones. It is said that they are lying in a kind of sleep, waiting for an external source of energy to revitalise them, and they are also said to be the very embodiment of evil, with a tremendous drive to destroy those who disturb them.

One day, in 1996, during the massive excavations across the Berkshire countryside for the controversial Newbury bypass, an enormous bulldozer overturned for no apparent reason and its driver was seriously injured. Green activists, of whom there were many at the site, tunnelling and making tree houses to hamper the work, were immediately suspected of sabotaging the vehicle, but investigators determined that no human agency had been involved in the incident. There were two groups of four dents in the panels of the bulldozer, as if something with titanic strength had seized it with a huge pair of hands and pushed it over.

That same night a squad of twelve security guards who were patrolling the cyclone fences and enormous barbed-wire barriers of the excavation zone heard a frantic cry for help on their radios. The call came from a guard in a portakabin. The guard, named Steve, said something was attacking him, and the message from his radio receiver seemed garbled with interference. When the guards arrived at the scene, they found that the enormously heavy, 46-foot-long, mobile living-quarters unit had been turned on its side. Something had overturned the portakabin and had apparently bashed its walls in at the same time. A ladder was brought to the scene and three guards used it to gain access to the door of the tipped-over cabin, which was now on the top.

Inside, they found Steve writhing in agony with a broken collarbone and a sprained arm. He seemed really frightened, and clutched his torch in the darkness. He rambled on about a huge misty object with long arms that had risen out of one of the excavated pits and chased him. The guards told him to be quiet and carefully lifted him out of the overturned portakabin. Then something quite unbelievable happened. As the guards were slowly descending the ladder with Steve, one of the eight other security guards pointed to the huge, excavated hole and shouted: "Look! What's that?"

Reports differ about what exactly happened next, but it is said that a plume of vapour rose from the hole and materialised into a strange elongated figure with disproportionately long arms, which hovered in the air and moved threateningly towards the security men. Five Alsatians were unleashed and ordered to attack the vaporous entity. Three of the dogs immediately dropped dead in their tracks, and the other two yelped pitifully, and ran off with their tails between their legs.

The guards also fled when they saw the menacing thing drifting in their direction, and noticed that there was suddenly a lot of interference on their radios and mobile phones. The nebulous object was heard to buzz and crackle, as if it was composed of electrical energy. Two guards who were closest to the apparition described how it had two twinkling spots of yellow light which looked like a pair of eyes.

It is alleged that a governmental committee sanctioned a team of ghost busters and even a Church of England vicar to identify, and hopefully exorcise, the ghost from the site, but the cleric and the paranormal researchers both agreed that the thing that had scared the wits out of the security guards was not a normal ghost of a dead person – but a powerful spirit of something that had never lived as a human. Research uncovered that even the Saxons had regarded the place where the thing had been seen as a taboo area for some reason. The vicar was of the opinion that the entity was extremely ancient, and advised the committee to fill in the pit from where the thing had been seen to emerge, as soon as possible.

The pit was duly filled in with earth that had been excavated from the same spot and, as yet, there have been no further sightings of the mighty, malevolent apparition.

Could the vapourous being have been a manifestation of one of the fabled Ancient Ones, who took refuge under the earth with Lucifer? And if not, what sort of malevolent being was able to strike terror into the hearts of twelve grown men and kill three big dogs without even touching them?

THE STRANGE SOLITARY SCIENTIST

History records that Sir Henry Cavendish, the English scientist and natural philosopher, was born in Nice in 1710, but the exact circumstances of his birth were said at the time to be bizarre – and some apocryphal sources say that a child substitution took place.

The great genius of the eighteenth century studied at Cambridge University, but decided to leave in February 1753 without earning a degree, because at that time, in order to be awarded a degree, students at the famous university had to declare that they were believing Christians and practising members of the Church of England. Cavendish was not prepared to lie, and admitted that he could see no logic in religion and so could not receive a degree.

Now for the first mystery regarding this unusual man. Despite having no degree, and without having written a single scientific paper, Sir Henry was warmly welcomed as a member of the prestigious Royal Academy of Science in 1760, at the age of 29. Cavendish's entry into the highly respected Academy was unprecedented, and no one has since entered the scientific fraternity without a degree.

Thirteen years after he became a member of the Academy, Cavendish suddenly became fabulously rich, literally overnight. The source of this vast wealth has never been traced – some contemporaries of the scientist thought the money was an inheritance, while others hinted that the fortune was accrued from an aristocrat as payment for a lucrative alchemical process that Cavendish had discovered. When Cavendish's bank heard of his newly-acquired wealth, his banker immediately wrote to him, advising him to invest the huge sum. Cavendish wrote back, warning the banker:

Sir, my private financial affairs are my own business. Kindly look after the sum of money I have already deposited with you. If you bother me again, I will take out all my money!

As far as his banker was concerned, Cavendish was wasting his money by giving it away to numerous charitable causes. For instance, one day

Cavendish heard that the young student who catalogued the books in his library was experiencing dire financial troubles, and immediately sent the young man a draft for ten thousand pounds sterling. An excessive gesture by anyone's standards!

This was by no means an isolated act of philanthropy. Cavendish literally gave away millions of pounds to hundreds of impoverished individuals – yet still had millions left in his coffers when he died. He bequeathed most of his riches – which included ownership of a canal and several grand buildings – to his distantly related heirs.

Upon his death it also transpired that Cavendish had been a principal stockholder of the Bank of England. But around the time that he acquired his mysterious wealth, his behaviour had become increasingly bizarre. He settled in London at a house in the street that nowadays bears his name, close to Clapham Common. At the rear of his house he had a stairway built which was meant to be used by the female staff. Cavendish apparently thought that women were an incompatible species, and the maids were given strict orders to stay out of his sight – if he chanced to bump into a female domestic at his house, he would fire her immediately. He shunned contact with almost everybody, and resorted to leaving his staff specific instructions regarding his well-being on written notes left on his hall table.

With virtually no interruptions, the solitary Cavendish could devote all his time to his remarkable scientific experiments. He made a number of breakthroughs in the field of chemistry, and even constructed an ingenious device that allowed him to calculate the weight of the earth. He also formulated a hypothesis about the deviation of light rays in the vicinity of the sun's mass. This theory was corroborated centuries later by Einstein's Theory of Relativity.

Cavendish also experimented with electricity, and long before Volta and Galvani, he told disbelieving colleagues at the Royal Academy of Science that electricity was the means by which the brain controlled muscles, and he also predicted that this mysterious force would change the world. But the scientific fellows at the Academy only laughed at the strange hermit. They thought that he was mad because he rejected Christianity in favour of Hindu philosophy, and eccentric because of the array of seemingly empty glass tubes that he was continually hoarding. In 1921, researchers discovered these tubes in Cavendish's laboratory and found them to be filled with rare inert gases.

One strange-looking tube containing argon had electrodes fitted at each end, suggesting that Cavendish had passed an electric charge through it to make the tube of gas light up like the modern neon-light tube. Another tube had elaborate mirrored electrodes inside, which suggests that he was on the brink of creating an argon laser. Fortunately, Cavendish did not let his prototype death-ray see the light of day in 1777. Perhaps he envisioned the horrific consequences of a laser-armed British Empire. The year 1777 was a turning point in the War of American Independence, and the battle of Stillwater would have had a very different outcome if General Burgoyne had deployed an argon laser cannon!

Sir Henry was also fascinated with space, and seemed to sink into a kind of hypnotic trance whenever he looked at the face of the moon. He would stare at the lunar disc for hours, perhaps with a burning desire to explore that beckoning globe. One night, during the Royal Society Club dinner, a crowd of scientists were looking out of a window, smiling and chatting about something that had caught their attention. Cavendish, who was seated on the other side of the room, presumed that the scientists were observing the moon, so he got up and joined them, only to see, to his disgust, that the learned men were enthralled with the sight of a beautiful young woman who was leaning out of a window in the house opposite. Cavendish turned abruptly and marched back to his seat with his jaw set and his head bowed.

Shortly before his death in March 1819, Cavendish rang a bell to summon his servant. When the servant arrived at his sickbed, Cavendish said, "Listen carefully to what I have to tell you. I'm going to die. When I am dead, but not before, go and tell Lord George Cavendish." The servant was shocked by this bald statement, and, concerned about the fate of his master's soul, presently returned to his bedside and nervously mentioned the administration of the last sacrament. Cavendish seemed puzzled by this suggestion and simply replied, "I don't know what you mean. Bring me some lavender water and come back when I am dead."

Within the hour, Sir Henry Cavendish was dead. In his will he left millions to his heirs, as well as a set of specific instructions regarding his interment. He recorded in his will that he should be buried in a specially-built vault in Derby Cathedral (without any examination or post-mortem). The vault was to be walled up immediately and no inscriptions were to be made to identify the tomb. These strange instructions were carried out by his heirs on 12 March 1810.

Today, we have hundreds of Sir Henry's papers written in a strange, symbolic shorthand which form but a rudimentary sketch of a peculiar individual who was seemingly born centuries too early. Where did a man who had no university degree get his extraordinary futuristic technological insights from? And, for that matter, why has no one ever been able to trace the source of Cavendish's incredible wealth? Hundreds of years after his death, the lonesome scientist still remains a fascinating enigma.

Is there Intelligent Life on the Moon?

According to present estimates, the moon was probably formed around the same time as the Earth and the other planets of the solar system, around 4,600 million years ago. During the first 700 million years the moon was bombarded by gargantuan rocks from space – the interplanetary debris left over from the solar system's formation. These impacts were responsible for the massive craters we now see in the NASA photographs of the lunar surface. It's thought that this continual bombardment in the moon's early history melted its outer crust, and that when the barrage of mountain-sized meteorites had diminished, the molten rock gradually cooled at the top and became solidified in the almost absolute cold of space. This solidified top stratum contains abundant traces of feldspar, zircon, pyroxene, olivine, aluminum, calcium and sodium, as well as small amounts of magnesium, iron, and even radioactive uranium.

There is also a surprising amount of oxygen contained in moonrock. If we treated two and a half tonnes of the stuff with a chemical reducing agent, it would release a tonne of oxygen – sufficient to keep a lunar settler alive for three years. Although oxygen and other gases are locked up in the lunar crust, the moon, unlike Earth, does not have any protective atmosphere, and so the surface is exposed to dramatic temperature extremes (-180°C in the shade to +110°C in direct sunlight).

In short, according to the astronomical textbooks, the moon is a hostile, airless globe, completely devoid of any life. But this doesn't seem to be the case at all when we take into consideration the hundreds of well-documented reports from astronomers and astronauts who have seen strange things on the surface of our closest celestial neighbour. Only in recent years has the term, 'transient lunar phenomena' (invented by the British astronomer Patrick Moore) been included in astronomy textbooks. Transient lunar phenomena, or TLP, is a term used by astronomers to label the host of strange objects that have been observed on the moon over the centuries.

One early example of TLP was recorded in the eighteenth century by William Herschel, the brilliant British astronomer who discovered the planet Uranus. On 18 August 1787, Herschel looked through his telescope and sighted a red sparkling glow on the dark half of the crescent moon that resembled 'slowly burning charcoal, thinly covered with ashes'. On 12 November that same year, two other astronomers witnessed bolts of lightning on the moon.

A little under a year later, on 26 September 1788, the German astronomer Johann Heronymus Schroter, saw a dazzling white point of light shining among the peaks of the lunar Alps near to the crater Plato, which lasted for 15 minutes. Seven further sightings of activity on the lunar surface by professional moon-gazers are noted in Volumes XXVI and XXVII of *The Philosophical Transactions of the Royal Society*. One of these controversial reports was penned by none other than the Astronomer Royal, the Reverend Nevil Maskelyne, who saw a strange cluster of lights moving across the dark half of the lunar disc.

In July 1821, the German astronomer, Franz Gruithuisen – the originator of the meteoric impact theory of lunar cratering – saw brilliant flashing points of light on the surface of the moon. When he announced that he had discovered a lunar city, his colleagues ridiculed him, and Gruithuisen burned the notes of his observations. Five years later, on the night of 12 April 1826, a professional astronomer named Emmet recorded a sighting of an enormous black cloud moving across the moon's Sea of Crises, or Mare Crisium.

Over half a century after this sighting, another odd lunar spectacle was observed by several independent astronomers: a 'luminous cable' which gradually stretched from west to east, until it completely spanned the crater Eudoxus. The line of light lasted for almost an hour, then blinked out.

Lights and clouds are not the only inexplicable things that have been seen on the moon. On 4 July 1881, two 'pyramidal protuberances' appeared on the moon's limb (the outer edge of the lunar disc), but as the world's most powerful telescopes were scrutinising these gigantic structures, they seemed to fade away. A year after this bizarre 'mirage', moving and stationary shadows were sighted in the vicinity of the crater Aristotle. The shadows seemed to be cast by an enormous object that was difficult to make out because it was the same colour as the lunar crust.

On 31 January 1915, astronomers were shocked to see a luminous shape in the Littrow crater that resembled the Greek letter gamma. This same luminous shape was later spotted near the crater Birt, and an account of it was printed in the highly respected *Astronomical Register* in London.

Other 'glyphs' have been seen too. A radiant 'X' has been seen in the shadows of the crater Eratosthenes many times over the years, and a strange, glowing, chequered shape has been sighted in the Plato crater on more than one occasion.

In 1899, another mystery of lunar origin was created when the scientific genius Nikola Tesla began broadcasting high-powered radio signals into space from his laboratories in Colorado Springs. Seconds after the experimental broadcasts, the dials of Tesla's radio equipment began to register an intelligent sequence of radio signals. Tesla had heard the howls and static from the aurora borealis and solar disturbances, but the signals he now heard were clear and suggested a mathematical order. Furthermore, they were definitely not echoes of Tesla's original signals. Tesla pondered on the meaning of the signals, and later wrote, 'The feeling is constantly growing on me that I have been the first to hear the greeting of one planet from another.'

Besides Marconi, no one else in the world had the technology to broadcast such radio signals in 1899. Tesla initially suspected that intelligence on Mars was the culprit, but upon further consideration concluded that the speed of the reply to his own signals suggested somewhere much closer, and the moon seemed to be the only logical answer. A radio signal from the moon takes around one and a quarter seconds to arrive, whereas from Mars, because it is so far away, it takes up to 23 minutes.

Strangely enough, around the time Tesla was apparently receiving signals from an extraterrestrial source, Marconi was transmitting the letter 'V', in Morse code, to his assistants 50 miles away, when something inexplicable happened. Marconi also received a signal of unknown origin, which seemed to be in some sort of code similar to Morse.

He wrote down the mysterious message and saw that the code contained the Morse code for 'V', as if something was replying to his original transmission. Marconi believed the signal had been broadcast from space, but kept his opinion to himself for years. When he finally told the *New York Times* about the signals, the reaction of members of the public was to either be frightened, or amused, by the claims.

More unearthly signals were picked up at the dawn of the radio age. In the 1920s and early 1930s, mystifying radio bursts were received from the moon, the most spectacular signals being the ones received by Dr Van der

Pol in October 1929. Dr Van der Pol, of the Philips Research Institute at Eindhoven in Holland, had transmitted radio call-signs of different durations at 30-second intervals in September 1928. Three weeks after the transmissions, Van der Pol was flabbergasted to receive echoes of his original transmissions.

Curiously, something had happened to the original signals – they now contained delay intervals (in seconds) of 8, 11, 15, 3, 8, 8, 12, 15, 13, 8 and 8. More echoes of this transmission were received throughout February 1929 on radio sets all over the world, and the same transmission was picked up again in October 1929. It was even heard for the fourth time in the 1940s, all of which defies explanation. The Van der Pol echoes suggest that the original message had been intercepted, interpreted and re-broadcast by something out in space. The general consensus in the 1930s was that the signals were of lunar origin.

In July 1953, a spectacular change occurred on the moon's surface that was witnessed by astronomers all over the world. An enormous 'bridge-like structure', of over 12 miles in length, was seen stretching across part of the Sea of Crises. John J O'Neil, the former science editor of the *New York Herald Tribune* was one of the first to see it, and he was at a loss to explain it, because no astronomer had sighted such a bridge before. Another witness to the strange spectacle was the eminent British astronomer and lunar expert HP Wilkins, who was interviewed by BBC Radio about the bridge. He struck fear into listeners by remarking, "It looks artificial. It looks almost like an engineering job. It's very straight and definitely solid, as it casts a shadow."

The bridge across the Sea of Crises is now nowhere to be seen. It has vanished as mysteriously as it appeared.

In 1956, a year before the start of the Space Race, radio telescopes around the world reported a code-like chatter coming from the moon. In October 1958, the same radio emissions were heard, but on this occasion, the culprit was spotted by American, British and Soviet astronomers through optical telescopes as well. A small globular object was spotted whizzing towards the moon at 25,000 miles per hour. Some astronomers said the object was a meteorite, but that such an object would not have been able to transmit high-powered radio signals.

Ten years later, on 21 December 1968, two more unidentified interplanetary objects were tracked by the optical and radio telescopes of the world. The two saucer-shaped objects in question were apparently accompanying Apollo VIII as it orbited the moon. It is alleged that Borman, Lovell and Anders – the three astronauts on board Apollo VIII – saw the UFOs at close quarters, and also heard weird, unintelligible voices which broke in on the special channel used to communicate with mission control. The UFOs later darted away from the American spacecraft and descended towards the lunar surface. It has been alleged for many years that most of the astronauts on the Apollo missions encountered UFOs on and around the moon, but NASA has always strenuously denied the claims. All the same, manned and unmanned lunar exploration has produced many unanswered questions.

A year after Apollo XI had landed on the moon, the following article appeared in the *Daily Telegraph* on 10 July 1970.

From our New York Staff
Photographs of the lunar surface have revealed objects that appear to have been placed there by intelligent beings, it was claimed yesterday.
Mysterious spires on the Moon were said to have been revealed by Russia's Luna 9 and America's Orbiter 2 spacecraft four years ago.
The claims were made in the Argosy magazine, which said the Russian and American spacecraft had photographed groups of solid objects at two widely separated locations.
The two groups of objects are arranged in definite geometric patterns and appear to have been placed there by intelligent beings.
The photographs taken by Orbiter 2 showed what appeared to be the shadows of eight-pointed spires shaped like Cleopatra's Needle.

The Russians believed that their probe, Luna 9, had photographed some sort of monument, but NASA wouldn't confirm this verdict. The spires stood in the Ocean of Storms in a formation almost identical to the 'abaka' alignment that the ancient Egyptians used. In fact, the spires were arranged in precisely the same way as the three great Egyptian pyramids on Earth.

After studying TLP for decades, two Russian scientists, Mikhail Vasin and Alexander Shcherbakov, came to the controversial conclusion that the moon was an artificial satellite of the Earth that had been put into orbit about our planet at some time in the distant past by intelligent beings from another solar system. This unusual hypothesis was instantly dismissed as nonsensical by the international scientific community, but unknown to the two Russian freethinkers, a much-respected American astronomer and astrophysicist named Morris Jessup had come to the conclusion in the 1950s that the Moon was a base for UFOs. Jessup too had scoured astronomical records for references to lights and other strange phenomena seen on the moon, and noticed that the strange lunar activity corresponded with UFO activity on Earth. He published his theories in 1955, but no one took him seriously. Some naturally regarded him as a crank, but this 'crank' had discovered many double stars, and as well as teaching astronomy and mathematics at Drake University, had erected and supervised the largest refractor telescope in the southern hemisphere for the University of Michigan.

Alas, in 1959, Jessup was found dead in his estate wagon in Dade County Park, Florida. A hose leading into the car had been attached to the exhaust pipe. It looked like suicide, but close friends of the scientist strenuously argued that Jessup was not the sort of person who would kill himself, and shortly after his death there were rumours that he had been disposed of by sinister individuals because he had found out too much about UFOs. Strangely enough, shortly before his untimely death, Jessup had announced that he had made a breakthrough regarding the UFO problem.

According to Vasin and Shcherbakov, the Moon would be found to be a hollow metal sphere which housed enormous atomic engines and other mechanical workings. They also asserted that the metallic hull of the 'spaceship' moon – estimated to be about 40 miles thick – had been cratered by collisions with asteroids during its wanderings through the cosmos.

Oddly enough, there is now evidence which suggests that the moon does indeed have a metallic shell. This finding was made in November 1969, when several highly sensitive seismometers were set up by the Apollo XII astronauts on the moon's Sea of Storms to measure lunar tremors, or 'moonquakes'. Shortly afterwards, when the Lunar Module ascent stage had taken the astronauts back up to the orbiting Command Module, the astronauts sent the discarded ascent stage of the Lunar Module back down to the lunar surface. The disused spacecraft impacted into the moon's surface and was smashed to pieces. The shock wave from the impact was picked up from the lunar seismometers on the moon's surface, and when NASA scientists back on Earth heard the data transmissions, they couldn't believe their ears. The moon's crust was ringing like a gigantic bell, and continued to ring for nearly an hour. When all of the seismological data had been fed through the computers at Houston, NASA admitted that the Moon seemed to be behaving like a hollow sphere with a metallic layer some 30 to 40 miles deep.

NASA created more artificial moonquakes to retest their lunar seismometers in April 1970, when the spent third stage of the Saturn V booster rocket, from the ill-fated Apollo XIII, was sent crashing into the moon. The booster rocket hit the lunar surface and exploded with a force equal to 11 tonnes of TNT, just over 87 miles from the site where the seismometers had been set up. Again, the moon's crust emitted a ringing sound, this time for an incredible duration of 90 minutes. NASA rechecked the seismological data, and again established that the data indicated that the moon had a metal shell.

The moon held another surprise for the Apollo programme. The orbits of spacecraft about the moon were often distorted by areas of the lunar surface where the moon's gravity field was particularly intense. NASA called these puzzling high-gravity areas 'mascons' – short for mass concentrations. What causes these mascons is still a mystery.

Even today, in these post-Apollo times, the moon remains a mysterious place. There is still no consensus regarding its origin, or age, and strange lights and other inexplicable phenomena are still regularly seen on the lunar surface. In 1996, it was reported that the Pentagon had sent a number of military probes to the moon in the late 1980s and early 1990s. There were rumours that the US military had been testing nuclear weapons on the lunar surface, but the Pentagon furiously denied the claims.

According to a February 1996 feature in Britain's *UFO Magazine*, the Pentagon's military lunar probes had been sent to photograph strange structures on the moon from close quarters with complex hi-tech cameras. The magazine published an astonishing photograph of a tower-like object on the moon's surface near the crater Ukert, estimated to be over two miles in height. The photograph had allegedly been leaked from the Pentagon's files and sent to the public via the Internet. It is claimed that the tower, which is said to be nicknamed 'the Shard' by Pentagon officials, was constructed by UFO occupants who use the moon as a base, but as expected, the US military denies that the photograph was sent back by their probes. What then, is the purpose of the Pentagon's lunar probes? That information is still classified, say the officials in the US Defence Department – leaving us to speculate just what secrets the moon still holds.

THE MAN WHO COULDN'T BE HANGED

For ten years, James Berry of Yorkshire was a police constable, and during that time he made many friends and many enemies. One acquaintance of the Yorkshireman was William Marwood, an old executioner from the City of London, who liked to give Berry a blow by blow account of the techniques he employed to hang criminals.

When Marwood died in 1883, 32-year-old Berry decided that the police force was no longer for him, and finding himself desperate for a vocation in life, opted for the macabre career of hangman. With all the knowledge of the gallows obtained from Marwood, Berry confidently applied for his deceased friend's job, but was turned down. But the ex-policeman persisted with his unusual aspiration, and was eventually rewarded when he received his first commission, to hang two men at Calton Prison in Edinburgh, for which he was to receive 21 guineas. Included in the commission was a second-class return rail ticket from Berry's hometown of Bradford, and money for board and lodgings.

On the night before James Berry was due to hang the men, he had a vivid nightmare about his new occupation. In the dream, he found that he could not hang a man because the trapdoor on the gallows refused to open. This same disturbing dream returned to haunt Berry's sleep many times over the years.

However, the following morning everything went smoothly, and the two condemned men were dispatched without any problems.

On the night of 15 November 1884, Miss Emma Whitehead Keyse, a former maid of honour, and friend of Queen Victoria, was found battered to death with her oil-soaked clothes ablaze at a villa known as 'The Glen', in Babbacombe, Devon. Miss Keyse's cook, Elizabeth Harris, discovered the body of her mistress in the dining room, after waking in her own smoke-filled room. She said that Miss Keyse's head had been battered in, and her clothes doused in oil from a lamp evidently lit by the murderer. After taking a statement from the cook, the police quizzed the dead woman's other servant, a 19-year-old footman named John Lee, who was the half-brother of Elizabeth Harris.

Lee had a reputation as a petty thief and had only been hired by Miss

Keyse out of pity. With such a track record, the footman soon became the prime suspect in the eyes of the police, despite the fact that he had tried to put out the fire on the night of the murder, and had broken down in tears upon hearing that his mistress had been murdered, saying, "I have lost my best friend," to the village constable, who was first to arrive at the scene of the crime.

But the police painted a different picture and relied on the large body of circumstantial evidence that was building up against the teenager. Lee had bloodstained clothing, and an empty can that had contained lamp oil was found in the pantry where Lee had been seen shortly before the fire broke out. Lee tried to explain. He told the police that the blood on his clothing was his own, from where he had gashed his hand while breaking a window pane to let out the smoke from the fire, although he couldn't explain the empty can of lamp oil.

Lee was arrested and charged with murder, and at his subsequent trial, the prosecution made it clear that John Lee, and only John Lee, had sufficient motive. Just before her brutal death, Miss Keyse had cut Lee's weekly wages of four shillings in half, because he had come under suspicion of theft, so the prosecution alleged; Lee had therefore killed her in fit of anger.

Lee protested his innocence, but his pleas fell on deaf ears and the jury reached a guilty verdict. Shortly before the sentence was passed, Lee declared from the dock, "I am innocent. The Lord will never permit me to be executed!"

The judge sentenced John Lee to death by hanging.

After the trial, a rumour circulated that Miss Keyse had discovered Lee's half-sister, Elizabeth Harris, making love with a man in bed. Being a rather prim, puritanical individual, Miss Keyse was allegedly outraged and took a swipe at the naked couple, and out of sheer panic, Miss Harris had struck back at her frail mistress with her fist, killing her outright. The rumour went that Miss Harris and her lover then took Miss Keyse's body to the dining room, where they battered the dead woman's skull in order to create the impression that a violent murder, perpetrated by an intruder, had taken place. Miss Harris realised that the police wouldn't be so easily fooled, so she sprinkled the contents of a can of lamp oil over the corpse and set fire to it, hoping that the flames would make the cause of Miss Keyse's death hard to determine.

But the improvised cremation attempt didn't succeed, because John Lee was alerted by the smell of burning and ran into the dining room with a pail of water to douse the flames. As he did so, either Elizabeth or her lover placed the incriminating can of lamp oil in the pantry where Lee had been working.

On the night before the execution Lee chatted in his cell with the prison governor and the chaplain, and the former told the condemned man that there was no chance of a reprieve. Lee responded by shrugging resignedly, then said, "Elizabeth Harris could say the word which could clear me, if she would."

When the governor and the chaplain left the cell, Lee settled down and had no difficulty sleeping. The dream he had was a strange one. He dreamed he was standing on the gallows with the noose around his neck, but the trapdoor wouldn't open, despite the hangman's repeated yanks on the lever. When Lee awoke from the dream, he felt that God had assured him that there was nothing to worry about, as he would not die on the gallows.

Shortly before eight o'clock on the morning of Monday 23 February 1885, James Berry led John Lee to the centre of the trapdoor on the gallows, then proceeded to strap Lee's legs together below the knees, before positioning and tightening the rope around his neck. Berry pulled the white hood over the doomed man's head, then walked to the lever. After a short, tense pause, Berry threw the lever – and the expected sound of bolts being drawn below the gallows was heard. Death was now only a heartbeat away for Lee, but, to everyone's amazement, the trapdoor on which he was standing refused to open. Berry's recurring nightmare had come true – and Lee's dream also.

Berry trembled, horrified, cold beads of sweat breaking out on his forehead. Trying to preserve a professional air, he took the hood and noose off Lee and tested the stubborn trap with a sandbag that weighed exactly the same as him. The trapdoor opened without a problem, and the sandbag crashed to the ground under the gallows.

Lee was then manoeuvred onto the trap again with the hood over his head and the noose re-positioned around his neck. This time, all the witnesses to the impending execution were sure that the trap would work.

Berry pulled the lever – but again the trap beneath Lee's feet stayed stubbornly shut.

Berry's face started to twitch with anxiety, and with shaking hands he again took the noose and hood off Lee, and guided him off the trap.

A prison engineer and Berry discussed the problem, and a carpenter was summoned. When the edges of the trap had been planed, and the bolts of the hanging apparatus thoroughly greased, a sandbag was again tested as a substitute for Lee, who by this time must have been suffering mental torture, even though his dream seemed to be coming true. Everything went like clockwork – the sandbag fell like a stone.

Lee was put on the trap for the third time. The hooded man stood there, waiting for Berry to throw the lever. Berry inhaled the cold morning air, then pulled the lever as hard as he could. The chaplain looked away as the greased bolts slid across as expected, but to his total astonishment, he saw that Lee was still standing on the unopened trap. The chaplain fainted, but was caught by a warder before he could hit the floor. It was decided that a messenger should be sent to London to inform the Home Secretary of the botched hanging attempts. While everyone waited for the messenger to return, Lee was asked if he felt like eating a last breakfast, and he consumed a substantial meal.

It was the hangman, James Berry, who could not stomach the meal – so Lee ate Berry's meal as well!

About nine hours later, the messenger returned from London to inform Lee that he had been granted a reprieve by the Home Secretary – the death sentence would be commuted to life-imprisonment.

In the event, Lee was released after serving 20 years. He came out in 1905 and married his childhood sweetheart who, incredibly, had waited patiently for his release, convinced of his innocence. The couple emigrated to America, and up until his death in 1933, John Lee, the man who couldn't be hanged, swore that he was not a murderer. Whenever people asked him what he thought about being spared from the rope three times in a row, Lee refused to that say that it wasn't luck, or freak mechanical failure that had saved his neck – but divine intervention.

WHAT WAS THE FATE OF BRITAIN'S SPY DIVER?

In 1956, Lieutenant Commander Lionel 'Buster' Crabb dived with Royal Navy frogmen in the Scottish Isle of Mull's Tobermory Bay, in search of a payship of the Spanish Armada named *Duque de Florencia*. The ship had reputedly been sunk with £30 million of gold on board in 1588. However, it turned out that most of the treasure was missing, and all Crabb recovered was a number of worthless trifles. The 46-year-old underwater expert was amused with one particular prize from the sunken Spanish Galleon: a shrunken skull. Experts analysed the grisly relic and determined that it had belonged to a North African woman who had used it in black magic rituals. Crabb's friends urged him to get rid of the skull, fearing it would bring bad luck, but Crabb thought they were being ridiculous. Imagine how these friends reacted when, a little over a year later, in June 1957, they learned that Crabb's body had been found floating in Chichester harbour – minus its head. To shed some light on the sinister incidents that led to this bizarre death, we must look into Crabb's background.

Crabb was born in 1910. During his twenties he went through a succession of jobs, the last one, before the outbreak of the Second World War, as a merchant marine apprentice. While most lives were shaken by the advent of the war, Crabb saw it as an incredible opportunity to find a new direction in life. He began his career in the Royal Naval Patrol Service, and after quickly acquiring a commission, he was appointed as a bomb and mine-disposal expert with the Royal Navy at Gibraltar in 1942. Crabb had the unenviable duty of removing sensitive limpet mines which had been fixed to the hulls of Royal Navy merchantmen by Italian saboteurs.

Disposing of a bomb on terra firma requires great skill and courage, but underwater, the hazards are even greater. Nevertheless, Crabb excelled at his work, and was subsequently awarded the highly coveted George Cross medal and promoted to lieutenant commander. He was also awarded the Order of the British Empire. During this period, Crabb injured his left leg while on a dive, and the minor accident left him with a small, but distinctive scar. This scar would later be the subject of much debate at the inquest of a corpse that the coroner would claim was Crabb's.

While most of the world rejoiced at the end of the war in 1945, Crabb found himself confronted with an uncertain future. He felt he was no longer needed, and over the next ten years, often talked of suicide to his closest friends. His depression reached an all-time low in 1955 when he officially retired. He sought solace in constant drinking, and became something of a bore, reiterating the same stories over and over again of his undersea exploits. He was also an eccentric who preferred to wear his rubber wetsuits under his normal clothing, even his pyjamas.

In 1956 he jumped at the opportunity to work again and dive on the wreck of the *Duque de Florencia*, but further diving assignments were sporadic. Short of money, he reluctantly turned to working as a rep for a firm which sold catering equipment to coffee bars. Around this time, something quite unexpected happened, the details of which can never be fully known, but what *is* known is that Crabb was approached by someone working in the intelligence service. Who this agent was is still a matter of much conjecture, but what follows is a summary of the clandestine events that led to Crabb's disappearance under highly suspicious circumstances.

On 17 April 1956, Crabb booked into the Sallyport Hotel in Portsmouth, accompanied by Bernard Sydney Smith, an agent of Britain's Special Intelligence Service (SIS). Crabb pretended to be on business when he and Smith signed the hotel register, but Smith rather blatantly described his occupation as 'attached Foreign Office' – a somewhat clichéd cover for MI6 operatives.

According to Chapman Pincher, a respected authority on defence intelligence, Ted Davies, another MI6 officer was also involved, and shortly after dawn on the morning of 19 April, he escorted Crabb to a jetty a mere 200 yards or so away from the 12,000-tonne destroyers. They had been anchored in Portsmouth Harbour for just a day, and had brought over the Soviet Premier Nikolai Bulganin and Nikita Khrushchev, First Secretary of the Communist Party in the USSR, on a mission of goodwill in Britain. The British Prime Minister, Sir Anthony Eden, seeing the visit as a way of reducing the East-West tensions that existed during the Cold War, had issued a directive from Downing Street to all the intelligence services in Britain, banning any spying missions relating to the Russian ships, because discovery would obviously have a devastating effect on

Britain's tentative relations with the Soviet Union. The seasoned officers in the SIS thought this directive was unfair and unrealistic; whenever British warships docked at Leningrad, shoals of Russian spy divers would unashamedly examine the hulls of the ships for 'routine inspection purposes'.

Despite Eden's directive, MI6 had already installed highly sensitive microphones in the rooms of Claridges Hotel, where Bulganin and Krushchev were to stay, and extra surveillance had been set up in a neighbouring building.

At the jetty in Portsmouth Harbour, Crabb emerged from the freezing waters after his initial dive, which had lasted just a couple of minutes, for an extra pound of ballast weight. He complained of having trouble with his breathing apparatus, which was Royal Navy issue, but quite unsuited for diving below depths of 33 feet. Crabb said he'd had to surface during the operation, to purge his system of excess poisonous carbon monoxide. He then made another dive, but Davies never saw him alive again.

Later that day, Rear-Admiral VF Kotov, the Commander of the Soviet flotilla, told Philip Burnett, the Chief of Staff of the Portsmouth base, that Soviet sailors had spotted an unidentified frogman surfacing near the ships. Burnett, who maintained that he knew nothing of any surveillance operation, dismissed the Soviet's complaint, but shortly afterwards, James Thomas, the First Lord of the Admiralty, also saw the mystery frogman off the bows of the chief Russian ship. He made enquiries to Downing Street, but the ministers there could offer no explanation.

On 29 April, the *Ordzhonikidze* and the destroyers left Portsmouth Harbour and headed for home, and the following day, the Admiralty issued a controversial statement which caused a Parliamentary storm. The statement said that Crabb was presumed dead after failing to return from 'a test-dive in connection with trials of certain underwater apparatus in Stokes Bay – three miles from Portsmouth'.

Journalists refused to believe that an expert diver of Crabb's calibre had strayed three miles off course, and they descended on Portsmouth to investigate the real events behind the statement. The newshounds discovered that the head of Portsmouth CID had visited the Sallyport Hotel where Crabb had been staying and ripped out the incriminating pages of the hotel register. This fuelled speculation that Crabb had been spying on the Soviet ships, and when the Kremlin officials heard the rumour, they demanded an explanation from Britain's Foreign Office. The government had no choice but to admit that the frogman seen near their ships during their stay at Portsmouth Harbour had been Lionel Crabb. However, Eden stressed that Crabb had been operating without government permission, and assured the Soviets that disciplinary action was being taken against those who had staged the operation.

During a debate on the affair in the House of Commons, John Dugdale, the MP for West Bromwich, asked the Prime Minister for more information on Crabb's covert activity, but tantalisingly, Eden replied that such information "would not be in the public interest".

Where had Crabb disappeared to? This was another mystery. Some believed that the diver had been intercepted by Soviet frogmen who had taken him to a chamber in the *Ordzhonikidze* below the waterline, known as the 'wet compartment'. Crabb had probably then been confined and taken back to the Soviet Union to be interrogated and tortured. Some even believed that Crabb had been some sort of double agent who had gone over to the 'Red Navy'.

Fourteen months later, on 9 June 1957, the corpse of a man in a wetsuit was found by fishermen in the mouth of Chichester Harbour, just a few miles east of Portsmouth. The body had been decapitated, and the hands were also missing, but curiously, upon the left leg of the corpse there was a scar which looked identical to Crabb's wartime scar. The wetsuit was also of the same Italian make that Crabb favoured, but what proof was there that the corpse was the body of the missing frogman? Despite the deliberate removal of any substantial identification factors, the Chichester coroner confidently recorded a verdict that the body was that of Crabb. The British authorities seemed pleased with the verdict, and held the 'belief' that Crabb had died because of a combination of ill health and the inhalation of carbon monoxide from his closed-circuit oxygen.

Not long after the controversial inquest verdict, came a plethora of reports that Commander Crabb had been sighted in the Soviet Union living under a Russian alias. Patricia Rose, Crabb's fiancée, stated that she was convinced that the headless body was not Crabb's. She claimed that she'd had a message from a man who had met 'Crabbie' in Sebastopol, where he was allegedly training frogmen for the Russians. Rose said that the mysterious messenger accurately described the idiosyncratic way Crabb smoked and coughed.

The Labour MP Bernard Floud also fanned the controversy when he claimed that he had learned through a contact in MI6 that British Naval officers had actually witnessed the capture of Crabb.

Then, in 1968, Bernard Hutton published a fascinating book called *Commander Crabb is Alive*. Hutton states in the book that a Captain Roman Melkov of Leningrad told him that he had spoken to Crabb, and had a personal message from him for Patricia Rose. Melkov mentioned Crabb's pet name (Crabbie) as 'proof'. Melkov then went on to describe a conversation Crabb had had with an old diving companion named Sydney Knowles, just prior to his disappearance. Knowles later verified Melkov's story of his conversation with Crabb. At last, it looked as if there was a lead in the Crabb case.

However, on 8 May 1968, the body of Captain Melkov was found in the cabin of his ship *Kolpino*, which was anchored at London docks. He had shot himself. Not long afterwards, more curious reports were made. It was claimed that several sailors onboard the *Ordzhonikidze* had seen Crabb being escorted into the ship's hospital – which was later inexplicably sealed off during the vessel's return journey to the Soviet Union. While this rumour was circulating, a Russian forces magazine came to light in the West which carried a blurred photograph of a group of Soviet naval officers, and among them was a man who looked suspiciously like Commander Crabb – an underwater operations instructor named Lieutenant Lvev Lvovich Korablov. Crabb's ex-wife Margaret, and one of his old wartime friends inspected the photograph of 'Korablov' and both were convinced it was Lionel Crabb.

If Crabb did end up in the Soviet Union, why didn't the Russians make the fact public as a propaganda exercise? That remains an unanswered question today. Stranger still, the official government dossier on the Crabb case was not open to inspection within the normal period of the 30-year-rule, so the contents of the file are presumably still deemed to be too confidential. Perhaps one day we will be told more about the case of the vanishing spy diver.

THE TUNGUSKA ALIEN

Had the following unexplained incident occurred today, even in the slightly relaxed atmosphere of the post-Cold War, it would probably have triggered World War III. Fortunately, the greatest hammer blow from space to hit earth since prehistoric times happened when the twentieth century was barely eight-years-old. Even today, scientists are still at loggerheads regarding the nature of the extraterrestrial object which shook the world after exploding in the skies of pre-revolutionary Russia.

The momentous event happened at 7.15am local time on the last day of June 1908. At that precise moment, an object brighter than the morning sun ripped through the atmosphere over Siberia. A trainload of passengers on the Trans-Siberian railway stared in horror at the towering pillar of flame roaring through the clear blue skies at a phenomenal velocity of around a mile per second. The sonic boom given off by the sky invader rattled the railway track, convincing the engine driver that one of his coaches had been derailed. He jammed on the brakes, and as the train screeched to a grating halt, the mysterious fiery object thundered north. The quaking passengers listened in relief as the overhead danger gradually receded, and gazed out of the carriage windows at the great vapour trail suspended in the sky.

Almost 350 miles to the north of the train, the nomadic hunting tribes of the Evenki people felt the ground judder violently as they witnessed a cylindrical 'second sun' racing across the heavens. By now, the immense apocalyptic object had changed course, as if it was being controlled or steered. After passing over the terrified travellers, the object made a 45° right turn and travelled 150 miles before performing an identical manoeuvre in the opposite direction. The tubular-shaped object then proceeded for another 150 miles before exploding, with enormous violence, over the Tunguska valley.

The detonation occurred at a height of five miles, and the twelve and a half megatonne explosion (it might have even been 30 megatonnes), destroyed everything within a radius of 20 miles. Herds of reindeer were incinerated as they stampeded away from the explosion, and all other wildlife in the area was ignited by the searing heat blast. Thirty-seven miles from the explosion, the tents in which the frightened Evenki people had taken refuge were lifted high into the air by the resulting atmospheric shockwave, and their horses bolted off in terror, dragging their ploughs behind them.

At the centre of the explosion, a monstrous mushroom cloud rose steadily over Siberia. Such an horrific and truly devastating sight would not be witnessed again for another 37 years, until Hiroshima and Nagasaki. But this explosion was even fiercer than the A bombs which were dropped on those Japanese cities. The blast from the Tunguska explosion felled trees for 20 miles around as if they were matchsticks, and set entire forests alight. The shockwave generated by the mysterious cataclysm travelled twice around the world, and shook the recording pens of the microbargraphs at three meteorological stations in London, where they were interpreted as seismic jolts from some distant earthquake.

At a distance of 400 miles from the epicentre of the Tunguska blast, the relentless shockwave showed no signs of abating and knocked fishermen from their boats on the River Kan. The blast then deteriorated into a hurricane-like storm, and a strange black rain started to fall over the Tunguska valley. Days later, strange scabs started to break out on animals that had been too far away to be directly burnt by the blast, and a few weeks later, curious local investigators who had ventured to the site of the explosion, became sick and complained of strange burning sensations within their bodies. Were these perhaps signs of radiation sickness? But what meteoric object could be radioactive? Stranger still, why was there no crater at the site of the explosion? (All meteorites leave a crater.) And how could a meteorite travel horizontally for hundreds of miles and change course twice? Other strange occurrences seemed to suggest that the object which had exploded over Siberia was not a meteorite at all, but perhaps some nuclear-powered spacecraft from another world which had been forced to make an emergency crash-landing in a remote area of our world.

The first reports of a strange glow in the sky came from Europe. Shortly after midnight on 1 July 1908, Londoners were intrigued to see a pink phosphorescent night sky over the capital. People who had retired, awoke confused as the strange pink glow shone into their bedrooms like a mock dawn. The same ruddy luminescence was reported over Belgium. The skies over Germany were reported to be bright green, while those over Scotland were of such an incredible intense whiteness that they tricked the wildlife into believing it was dawn. Birdsong started and cocks crowed – at 2am. The night skies over Moscow were so bright that photographs were taken of the streets without using a magnesium flash. The captain of a ship on the River Volga said that he could see vessels on the river two miles away by the uncanny astral light and a golf game in England went on until almost 4am under the nocturnal glow.

In the following week, *The Times* newspaper was inundated with letters from readers all over the United Kingdom reporting the curious 'false dawn'. A woman in Huntingdon wrote that she had been able to read a book in her bedroom solely by the peculiar rosy light. There were hundreds of letters from people reporting identical lighting conditions after the Tunguska explosion. Scientists and meteorologists also wrote to the newspaper giving their opinions about the cause of the strange glare, which ranged from the Northern Lights to dust in the upper atmosphere reflecting the rays of the sun below the horizon. No one connected the phenomenon with the strange object which had exploded with the fury of an H-bomb in Siberia. Even the national press in Russia failed to mention the catastrophic event in the Tunguska valley, because the country was then entering a period of major political upheaval.

A serious investigation of the Tunguska incident did not take place for another 13 years, when a Soviet mineralogist named Leonid Kulik led an expedition to the site of the explosion. However, during those 13 years strange whispers and rumours spread across Siberia. There were tales of a strange being wandering the remote forests of Tunguska near the scenes of devastation. The nomadic reindeer herdsmen of Siberia sighted the gigantic grey humanoid figure some 50 miles north of the Chunya river. They saw the creature, who seemed to be over eight feet in height, picking berries and drinking water from a stream. The superstitious Mongol herdsmen regarded the freakish-looking stranger as one of the fabled Chuchunaa race of hairy giants, similar to the abominable snowman, who were said to inhabit the region. The nomads crept through the forest to get a better look at the figure, and they observed that the grey colour of the man was not hair but tattered garments of some sort. The herdsmen sensed that there was something unearthly about the being, so they retreated back into the forest and moved away from the area.

There were several more sightings of the grey goliath throughout the following 30 years, and each report indicated that the entity from the cold heart of Siberia was moving westwards. Alas, all accounts of the strange giant were interpreted as mere folklore tales of the Russian peasants.

In February 1927, Leonid Kulik went in search of the strange object which had exploded above Tunguska. He had read countless old newspaper clippings on the Siberian explosion and had conjectured that the object responsible for the widescale destruction had been a large meteorite composed of stone and iron. Being a mineralogist, Kulik looked forward to obtaining samples of the meteorite for analysis. He left the Trans-Siberian railway at the Taishet station, and on horse-drawn sledges, Kulik and his men set off on an arduous three-day odyssey through 350 miles of ice and snow until they reached the village of Kezhma, situated on the River Angara.

At the village, Kulik and his party of researchers replenished their supplies of food and then struggled on for a three-day journey across wild and uncharted areas of Siberia until they reached the log cabin village of Vanavara on 25 March. Kulik then tried to make headway through the untamed Siberian forests (or taiga as the Russians call it), but was forced to turn back after heavy snowdrifts almost froze the horses to death.

For three days Kulik was forced to remain in snow-bound Vanavara, but during this period he interviewed many of the Evenki hunters who had witnessed the Siberian fireball's arrival on the planet. Tales of the sky being ripped open by a falling sun and of a great thunder shaking the ground made Kulik even more eager to penetrate the taiga to find his Holy Grail. When the weather gradually improved, Kulik set out for the Tunguska valley and when he finally reached the site of the mysterious explosion, he was almost speechless. From a ridge overlooking the scene, Kulik took out his notebook and scribbled down his first impressions of the damage wreaked by the cosmic vandal. He wrote,

> *From our observation point no sign of forest can be seen, for everything has been devastated and burned, and around the edge of the dead area, the young, 20-year-old forest growth has moved forward furiously, seeking sunshine and life. One has an uncanny feeling when one sees 20 to 30-inch giant trees snapped across like twigs, and their tops hurled many yards away.*

Kulik then proceeded towards the felled forest, but two of the guides who had taken him and his assistants to the area refused to go any further. The guides told the bemused scientist that there was something, or someone, still lurking about in the area. Kulik thought the guides were superstitious fools, but they told him that a strange monster had been seen at twilight roaming the shadows of the dead taiga. The guides returned home and Kulik, fortunately, met a few bold members of the Evenki tribe who took him and the researchers further into the taiga. By June, Kulik and his men had reached the middle of the explosion site, where uprooted trees were scattered from the centre of the blast like the tangled spokes of a wheel. But there were no signs of a crater. Kulik then realised that the explosion had occurred above ground. The Evenki tribesmen seemed to become very uneasy in the middle of the devastation zone and started to talk about a supernatural presence in the area. But Kulik didn't have time to listen to such irrational ramblings; he had limited time to collect data for his colleagues back home at the Russian Academy of Sciences.

There were three further expeditions to the site of the Tunguska explosion, headed by Kulik, but in 1941 Hitler attacked Russia. The 58-year-old Leonid Kulik volunteered to defend Moscow but was wounded by the Nazis. He was captured by German troops and thrown in a prison camp where he died from his wounds.

The next three expeditions to the Tunguska valley, in 1958, 1961 and 1962, were led by the Soviet geochemist, Kirill Florensky, who used a helicopter to survey and chart the blast area. Florensky's team sifted the soil in the area and discovered a narrow strip of dust which was of extraterrestrial origin. The dust consisted of magnetic iron oxide (magnetite) and minute glassy droplets of heat-fused rock. Florensky carefully checked the radiation levels at the site, but the only radioactivity present seemed to be from the fallout which had drifted into the area from distant Soviet H-bomb tests.

Scientists who examined Florensky's findings and the data from further investigations of the Tunguska explosion site began to postulate that a fragment of Comet Encke had collided with our planet and smashed into Siberia in June 1908. Today, some scientists have theorised that the blast was caused by a wandering black hole, or a chunk of anti-matter. However, one piece of curious evidence seems to vindicate the spaceship theory. At the site of the Tunguska blast, there is a strange irregular shape at the centre of the circle of damaged terrain. Scientists and geologists who have analysed the shape say it looks as if it was caused by something exploding within a cylinder. Comets are not cylindrical and they certainly do not travel horizontally across the ground making 45° turns!

And what of the fabled Chuchunaa creature? What became of him? The last known encounter of the grey giant took place in Daghestan in 1941. A Colonel VS Karapetyan and his troops were called out to investigate sightings by frightened villagers of an enormous 'beastlike' figure in the Buinaksk Mountains. The soldiers spotted what they regarded as a monstrosity and gave chase. They cornered the towering creature in a cave, and without making any attempts to communicate with him, they took aim with their rifles and opened fire. The creature fell dead with a loud echoing thud. Colonel Karapetyan later wrote an account of the confrontation with the unidentified and unarmed human-like creature,

> *He stood before me like a giant, his mighty chest thrust forward. His eyes told me nothing. They were dull and empty – the eyes of an animal. And he seemed to me like an animal and nothing more … a wild man of some kind.*

The creature's corpse was left to the scavenging birds and wild, mountain animals, and the colonel and his men left the mountains and concerned themselves with the task of defending Russia from the Nazis. The humanoid they had killed may simply have been one of those mysterious 'men-beasts', such as the Yeti or Bigfoot, but according to some of the peasants of the Buinaksk Mountains, the over-sized man wore ragged grey clothes. Is it therefore possible that the creature in the cave murdered by the military was the same being that had first been seen by the Evenki tribe near the scene of the Tunguska explosion? This leads us to a tantalising possibility – was it a marooned alien from another world, who had managed to eject itself from a damaged spaceship after steering the craft away from the inhabited areas of Siberia?

If this is true, what a sad and barbaric end for a visitor who might have been able to teach us so much.

ZODIAC

It has often been stated that if Jack the Ripper was at large today, the modern police would have no problem in capturing him – although their efforts in capturing the Yorkshire Ripper left much to be desired. The following story, which unfolds near San Francisco in 1968, further proves that, even in modern times, serial killers who strike regularly in a specific area can still evade capture.

On 20 December 1968, a woman was driving through California from Vallejo (just north of San Francisco), to Benica. As she came down Lake Herman Road – a lonely stretch of highway known locally as a lovers' lane – the woman came across a parked station wagon. Next to the vehicle, a body lay on the cold macadam and another one lay on the ground further down the road. The woman drove straight into town, called the police, and so began the baffling case of the so-called Zodiac murders.

The police established that the bodies in the road were those of two teenaged high school sweethearts. David Faraday, aged 17, had been blasted in the head inside the station wagon. His girlfriend, 16-year-old Bettilou Jensen, had evidently been running away from the gunman, but had been shot in the back five times as she fled. Robbery was naturally suspected as a motive, but the boy's wallet in his jacket pocket still contained cash. Furthermore, the girl had not been raped or interfered with in any way, so the police were naturally mystified and assumed the killer had carried out a motiveless double murder. Or perhaps the murderer had been an admirer of the girl, and had resented her involvement with Faraday, but even this theory seemed way off the mark when the killer apparently struck again in the following July.

A man with a gruff voice telephoned the Vallejo Police Department on 5 July 1969, to report a second double murder, and as before, the victims were a couple.

"I wish to report a double murder," said the anonymous caller. "If you go one mile east on Columbus Parkway, to a public park, you will find the kids in a brown car. They have been shot by a 9-mm Luger." The man then chillingly added, "I also killed those kids last year. Goodbye!"

Police converged on the scene of the crime just as the caller had directed them. In a car at the parking lot they found 24-year-old waitress Darlene Ferrin – the mother of a young child – dead from gunshot wounds. Next to her in the car was Michael Mageau, with blood spurting from a gaping bullet hole in his neck. Mageau had also sustained three other gunshot wounds, but was still alive and would later go on to make a full recovery. He was able to tell the police that shortly after he and Darlene had driven to the parking lot, a car had pulled up beside them. It then drove away but returned ten minutes later, again parking alongside the couple's car. An intense beam of light suddenly shone into the couple's car and dazzled them. Mageau couldn't be sure if it was the driver of the other car who had shone the light into his eyes, but he presumed that it was.

The driver then coolly walked up to the couple's car and started to shoot them both at point blank range. Despite the dazzling light, Mageau still caught a glimpse of their assailant and reported that he was white, around 25 to 30 years of age, stockily built, around five feet, eight inches in height, with a round face and wavy light brown hair.

On the first day of the following month, two San Francisco daily newspapers, and the Vallejo *Times-Herald*, received letters which began,

Dear Editor,
This is the murderer of the two teenagers last Christmas at Lake Herman and the girl on the 4th of July ...

The letter then went on to describe details of the crime, including the guns and type of ammunition used, which made it clear to the police that the writer was the killer and not some hoaxer. The letters were all signed with a curious symbol – a cross, super-imposed on a circle, which looked like the hairs of a gunsight. Someone later established that the symbol was actually an ancient astrological sign which represented the zodiac – an imaginary belt in space which encompasses 13 constellations ranging from Aries to Pisces.

Why did the killer use an astrological symbol? Was he a twisted astrology freak who carried out hideous crimes when his horoscope was favourable? Stranger still, the killer's letters also contained a weird-looking code made up from pictograms – letters and signs arranged in a complex cypher. The murderer stated in his letter that if the code was broken, it would reveal his identity. Military experts were brought in to the investigation to crack the code, but they failed, and so the police wondered if the killer was just teasing them with a random jumble of letters and signs which meant nothing. Just when the code was about to be dismissed, a teacher from Alisal High School in Salinas, Dale Harden, finally cracked the killer's cypher. Unfortunately, the chilling deciphered message did not reveal the identity of the psychopathic murderer, but it did throw some light on the sick, warped, fantasy world which he inhabited. The weird message read:

> *I like to kill people because it is so much fun. It is more fun than killing wild game in the forest, because man is the most dangerous animal of all. To kill something gives me the most thrilling experience. It is even better than sex. The best part will be when I die. I will be reborn in Paradise, and then all I have killed will become my slaves. I will not give you my name because you will try to slow or stop my collecting of slaves for my afterlife.*

Shortly afterwards, another letter to the newspapers began, 'Dear Editor, This is Zodiac speaking …' and the missive proceeded to accurately detail the murder of Darlene Ferrin and the wounding of Michael Mageau in the parking lot.

The police and press naturally expected more killings by Zodiac, and on September 27 of that year, a man with the same distinctive gruff voice telephoned the Napa Police Department to report a particularly cruel and savage murder. On this occasion, Zodiac had captured two students from Pacific Union College who had been innocently picnicking near Lake Verriesa. Police found the victims' car parked on the shore of the lake. Cecilia Shepherd and Bryan Hartnell were lying bound together in the vehicle, drenched in their own blood. The girl had died from a number of knife wounds. Hartnell had received six stab wounds but miraculously was still alive.

When the college student had recovered from his injuries, he gave a graphic account of the terrifying ordeal he had undergone. He told how he and Cecilia had been accosted by a pudgy-looking man who wore a black hood with eye slits in it. The hood resembled the type worn by mediaeval executioners. On this hood was the Zodiac's circle and cross symbol painted in white. Through the eye-holes, Hartnell could make out a pair of spectacles with black frames. He could also see wisps of the masked man's hair, which looked light brown. The killer carried a pistol and a knife, and he demanded money from them, saying that he was an escaped convict. He tied up the trembling couple and then calmly announced, "I'm going to have to stab you people".

Hartnell bravely volunteered to be stabbed in an effort to spare the life of Cecilia. The masked fiend obliged his request and thrust the long blade of his knife into Hartnell six times. But the nightmare wasn't over yet, because he then savagely plunged the knife into Cecilia's body, at which point he went completely berserk. The coroner later counted 24 knife wounds on the girl's corpse and realised that they formed a bloody cross. A fisherman who had been in the area while the frenzied attack was taking place, told the police that he had heard the girl's terrible screams. After the enraged butchery, Zodiac had evidently been composed enough to leisurely scrawl his symbol on the door of Hartnell's car with a felt-tip pen.

Detectives traced the telephone that Zodiac had used to notify them of the frenzied stabbing. It was a public callbox embarrassingly situated close to the Napa Police Headquarters. Forensic experts managed to lift three fresh fingerprints from the callbox, but were disappointed to discover that the prints matched none held in the police records. This meant that the detectives could only tell the newspapers that, as far as they knew, the Zodiac didn't have a police record, which was hardly a breakthrough!

A fortnight later, on 11 October, Zodiac struck again. In broad daylight, he shot 29-year-old taxi driver Paul Stine in the back of the head, killing him instantly. This gratuitous killing happened in the Nob Hill area of San Francisco, but on this occasion the police got their first useful description of the killer from witnesses who had seen Zodiac calmly walking away from the scene of the crime. Police discovered that Zodiac had made off with the taxi driver's wallet and a strip of fabric torn from the victim's shirt. Ballistics experts also recovered the bullet that had taken Stine's life and noted that it had been fired from the same pistol that had killed Darlene Ferrin.

On the following day, the *San Francisco Chronicle* received a letter from the killer which criticised the police for being incompetent, and ended with a shocking threat. Zodiac wrote:

> Schoolchildren make good targets. I think I shall wipe out a school bus one morning some time. Just shoot out the tyres, then pick off the kiddies as they come bouncing out.

To rule out the idea that the letter had been penned by a sick hoaxer, Zodiac had also enclosed a fragment of the bloody shirt he had torn from the murdered taxi driver.

Police escorted school buses throughout Zodiac's territory for weeks, but fortunately the killer failed to carry out his repugnant threat.

The murder of the taxi driver was the last known Zodiac murder, but the killer continued to give the police a headache for many years to come.

On 21 October 1969, the murderer manipulated the media in a most sensational way. He telephoned the Oakland police and sincerely stated that he would willingly give himself up if he could be represented by a top-notch lawyer. Zodiac named two particular maverick lawyers that he had in mind – Melvin Belli and F Lee Bailey. The serial murderer then stipulated that he would require a period of air-time on an early morning TV chat-show. Arrangements were made by the television executives, who regarded the request from Zodiac as a spectacular, once-in-a-lifetime ratings winner, and so, at 6.45am, the *Jim Dunbar Show* was broadcast to a record TV audience.

Thousands of viewers tuned in to the show, eager to hear the killer speaking live. Almost an hour later, the waiting was over. At 7.41am, a caller came on the line chatting to lawyer Melvin Belli. He had a soft, boyish voice and he claimed that he was the Zodiac killer. He explained that he killed because he suffered from blinding headaches, and then proceeded to discuss some of the murders. Police tried to trace the call, but Zodiac kept hanging up and telephoning the studio back from different locations. He called back a total of 15 times, and finally ended his 'performance' by agreeing to meet Belli in front of a certain store in Daly City. At long last it looked as if there was a chance of catching the killer and bringing him to justice. Alas, Zodiac failed to keep his appointment with the lawyer.

Shortly before Christmas, Belli received a letter containing another piece of the murdered taxi driver's shirt. Zodiac wrote:

Dear Melvin,
This is Zodiac speaking. I wish you a Happy Christmas. One thing I ask of you is this, please help me ... I am afraid I will lose control and take my ninth, and possibly tenth, victim.

He did not carry out his threat, as far as it is known, and it seemed as if Zodiac then retired from hunting his 'afterlife slaves' and nothing more was heard from him until 1971, when the killer wrote to the *Los Angeles Times*. The letter read:

If the blue menaces are ever going to catch me, they had better get off their fat butts and do something.

The letter was signed in the usual way with his astro-sign, but also included the number 17, followed by a plus sign.

And that seemed to be it. The years dragged by, and many detectives thought that Zodiac had either died, or was killing more and writing less. Then, in 1974, the San Francisco Police Department received another letter from him. The killer now boasted of killing 37 people. A police graphology expert confirmed that the handwriting was definitely Zodiac's. The media thought the latest claim was staggering but the police – fearing an hysterical outcry from the tax-paying public – played down Zodiac's atrocious claim as a 'slight exaggeration'.

The last word from the killer seems to have been in 1990, when the *New York Post* received a letter signed by Zodiac. The writer of the letter intimated that he was now at large in the Big Apple, and gave details of four unsolved murders in New York and other descriptions which could only have been known by the killer. The writer's claim of 'NYPD 0, Zodiac 9' may be an exaggeration, but some detectives in the city are keeping an open mind.

In 1975, Sonoma County Sheriff, Don Striepeke, fed all the murder records filed in the state attorney's office into a computer. The computer linked 40 murders to one particular killer because of the modus operandi, the geographical area, and the time window. When the sites of these murders were plotted onto a map of northern California and Washington state, the results were startling. In Washington state, the murder sites formed two large rectangles connected by a line. County Sheriff Striepeke researched the strange geometrical shape and discovered that the same shape had been used as an occult symbol by witches in England, during the late Middle Ages. The symbol represented the afterlife (a subject Zodiac was certainly obsessed with), and was painted on the hearth of homes where people had recently passed away, to speed their spirit into the hereafter.

Striepeke may have been onto something with his computer-aided analysis of Zodiac's murders, because it later came to light that, by the side of some of his female victims, the police had found strange collections of twigs and stones – arranged to form two small rectangles linked by a line!

The Riddle of the Russian Hell

Since the collapse of the old Soviet Union in 1989, many bizarre secret files of the KGB have been inspected by the intelligence services of both America and Britain. In 1990, one of these old files was faxed to the Dll Department of the Secret Service in Whitehall, London, but what the dossier contained was so extraordinary and unbelievable, that the data it contained soon leaked out. What follows is the essential information contained in the file.

In August 1989, a group of geologists from Moscow was sent to Siberia, where a Soviet oil drill had managed to bore a hole into the earth's crust, to what is still a record depth of over 12 miles (19.2 km). However, something was obstructing the revolving tip of the drill, and no one had any idea what it could be. Dr Dimitri Azzakov, a world authority on the earth's crust, had therefore been sent for. And he arrived at the site accompanied by a team of experts.

Azzakov ordered further drilling attempts to be stopped and requested 12 miles (19.2 km) of heat resistant electrical cable. He attached a sensitive microphone to the end of the cable and lowered it through the hollow shaft of the drill. The microphone was water-cooled and coated with thermo-insulation tiles similar to those used on the heat-shield of space-craft.

One hour later, in his trailer, which was cluttered with electrical hardware, Azzakov switched on a sensitive amplifier that was connected to the underground microphone. He expected to hear the cracking and groaning produced by the stresses and strains of molten rock under pressure, but what he and the other five people present actually heard was to haunt them for the rest of their lives. The microphone picked up what sounded like hundreds of human voices, screaming and yelling in pain. Azzakov taped the sounds, and was obviously baffled by these disturbing subterranean wailings.

"It sounds like people down there, but it obviously cannot be," Azzakov said to an ex-military officer who was now supervising the drilling operation.

At last, one of the men present had the courage to voice what was on everyone's minds.

"You know, if I were not an atheist, I would say we were listening to the sounds of Hell."

Azzakov laughed very nervously at the man's comments. He was deeply disturbed by the distressing sounds but, being a scientist, it was his job to try and explain them. He therefore ordered a heat-resistant camera from the Baikonur space centre. Azzakov was a widely respected scientist and had many resources at his disposal. Within three days, a military helicopter arrived at the remote drilling outpost carrying the special camera, which was identical to a space probe camera, designed to withstand the heat of Venus.

The camera was lowered down the shaft for over an hour and switched on. According to the incredible account signed both by Azzakov and an aeronautics engineer from the space centre, shimmering pictures of people, silhouetted against glowing rocks, could be seen. The figures were motionless and lying about on the incandescent rocks. Every few minutes a bright light was seen to move among them, but the light was always out of focus, but seemed to be under intelligent control.

The harrowing scenes were allegedly being videotaped, but unfortunately, three minutes into the recording, the camera malfunctioned and the microphone melted. A blast of steam rushed up through the hollow shaft and sent foul clouds of evil-smelling sulphur and choking fumes to the surface. The drill had to be disconnected because of insurmountable mechanical problems within the shaft, and the drilling operation was subsequently moved to another site in Siberia, hundreds of miles away.

Azzakov and the expert from the space centre were later interrogated by the KGB and warned to say nothing to anyone in Russia about the weird, inexplicable incident. The country was then still under crumbling Communist control, and atheism was the official line of the ruling party. Any rumour of the strange inferno under Siberia would probably have been construed by many as possible evidence that Hell was a reality. The case is still unexplained and will probably remain a mystery for some time yet.

The Frozen Woman

There are many sane and respected people around the world today who intend to have their bodies 'put on ice' when they die. Their frozen corpses will be stored in liquid nitrogen at a temperature of -196° C, until a future time when advances in medical technology will allow the deep-frozen dead to be resurrected. These attempts at cheating death through freezing are practical examples of the relatively young science of applied cryogenics. Members of the Cryogenics Society of California are pioneers in this field, and started freezing newly-dead bodies in 1967. There are now cryogenic storage societies starting up in other parts of the world.

Many scientists still regard the prospect of cryogenic immortality as improbable and unlikely, as it is still difficult, if not impossible, to freeze human tissue fast enough to avoid vital-cell destruction. This problem will undoubtedly be resolved in the not-too-distant-future, and already, rudimentary human embryos have been successfully frozen at sub-zero temperatures. Moral watchdogs are concerned at the pace of progress in cryogenics, and recent legislation in Britain has limited the period during which scientists can hold the embryos in cold storage.

We don't have to look to cryogenics to see examples of deep-frozen mammals – nature has already beaten us to it. In the summer of 1977, a perfectly-preserved specimen of a six-month-old baby mammoth was disinterred by a bulldozer in the Yakutsk republic of the former USSR. This baby mammoth, nicknamed Dinah, is over ten thousand years old.

In 1900, a larger Russian mammoth was found in Berezovka, standing upright in the Arctic permafrost. The frozen beast was so perfectly preserved by the sub-zero temperatures that the ancient buttercups it had been eating when it died, were still stuck to its tongue! No reason has ever been given to explain why the mammoth died so suddenly. It never had a chance to swallow the flowers and the beast seems to have been literally frozen in its tracks.

Human bodies that have been frozen naturally in Arctic conditions have been reported from time to time. In August 1984, scientists chipped through five feet of gravel and permafrost on Beechley Island, which is situated at the entrance to Canada's Wellington Channel. What the excavating scientists came upon was breathtaking – three graves containing the bodies of sailors who had died in 1846. One of the corpses was perfectly preserved. The body was subsequently identified as that of seaman John Torrington, a member of the ill-fated Franklin Arctic expedition.

Sir John Franklin had left England in 1845 on a mission to find the Northwest Passage, a long-sought sea route from the Atlantic to the Pacific by way of Canada's Arctic islands. The British government and its Admiralty were confident that Franklin would find the passage, and they gave him two ice-region ships named *Erebus* and *Terror*, which had been completely overhauled and refitted for the expedition. Franklin and his men perished in the Arctic Circle before they could find the Northwest Passage, but the fate of the ships is still unknown.

However, in 1851, the captain and crew of a brig named *Renovation* were astonished to see two full-sized ships perched on top of a huge iceberg in the North Atlantic. Two old seadogs on the *Renovation* identified the ships through a telescope – they were the frozen wrecks of *Erebus* and *Terror*. The nineteenth-century ice-bound wrecks were allegedly sighted once more in the early 1950s, still embedded in an iceberg.

There have also been more sinister reports of people frozen in ice. The following story was sent buzzing across the Internet in the late 1980s, and was even reported in a BBC Radio bulletin in Britain. According to the story, in March 1988, towards the end of the Cold War, a Russian destroyer was on manoeuvres in the North Atlantic (about 800 miles south of Iceland), when a lookout on the ship, using high-powered binoculars, spotted an iceberg on the horizon. There was nothing unusual about an iceberg being in that area of the ocean in March, but what excited the lookout was the curious dark spot he could see on the iceberg. As the iceberg floated nearer to the destroyer, the lookout zoomed in on the dark spot and sighed in disbelief; the dot was the figure of a woman lying on a ledge, covered in a thin layer of ice, like a frozen blanket. She was dressed in a black jacket and a long black dress and was lying on her back.

The captain of the destroyer immediately dispatched a motorboat to investigate. Two divers left the boat and swam over to the ledge of the iceberg to take a closer look at what was obviously the frozen corpse from some sea disaster. Three more men, including a physician, came off the ship and spent almost an hour freeing the body from the ice. The woman, who looked about 25-30 years old, was perfectly preserved except for one ankle, which was blackened by the tissue-destroying ice crystals. However, the out-dated clothes she wore indicated that she had been frozen for a very long time, perhaps 50 years or more. The corpse was put into a body bag and taken on-board the Russian destroyer, where it was put in refrigeration until the ship returned to the Soviet Union.

The corpse was then transferred to a military hospital in Leningrad and thawed slightly to just under room temperature. Even the lipstick on the woman's face appeared fresh, and she looked as if she was only sleeping. Then, suddenly, the woman's eyes flew open! It was probably a mere reflex action and not a sign of life, but although the blue eyes were slightly bloodshot, they were still animated. All of the scientists present recoiled in shock. The eyes then rolled upwards and the eyelids flickered, then closed. One report said that the scientists tried unsuccessfully to resuscitate the corpse by firing a high voltage current through its chest, but the lungs were full of ice and the other internal organs were damaged beyond repair.

In the pockets of the woman's coat, several papers and belongings were found. A brooch, a purse with old money that dated back to the early 1900s, and a number of documents which stated that the woman had been a passenger on the *Titanic* liner which had sunk after hitting an iceberg 350 miles southeast of Newfoundland in 1912. It was surmised that the woman had probably fallen, or jumped, overboard from the stricken vessel and had somehow been swept onto one of the icebergs drifting through the waters.

The story was reported in some Russian satellite states, but the Soviet Union allegedly hushed up the strange find because the Russian destroyer responsible for finding the ice-bound corpse had been involved in electronic eavesdropping on very-low-frequency broadcasts from American submarines.

According to further reports that leaked out of the crumbling USSR in 1990, scientists removed the frozen woman's ova cells and were attempting to clone her. Whether or not she has now been finally laid to rest we may never know.

IN THREE PLACES AT ONCE

The following weird incident happened in London in the 1980s. It was documented in a magazine and several newspapers but it has never been satisfactorily explained.

In October 1987, at 1.30am, Rita Carson, a divorced 39-year-old woman, was awoken by a frantic hammering on the front door of her home in Wimbledon. Rita lived alone with her dog, a podgy, shapeless, old Labrador named Cally, and she was naturally nervous when she heard the knocking at that hour in the morning. She went downstairs, put on a coat, picked up a poker from the fireplace, then peeped through the curtains of the bay window to see who was knocking at the door. It was a man, but because his back was turned, she couldn't see his face. Rita went into the hall and called out, "Who is it?"

"It's me – Alan," said the stranger on the doorstep.

Cally started barking when she heard the voice. Rita calmed the dog down and asked, "Alan? Alan who?"

"Your cousin Alan. Alan Warner," said the man.

Rita suddenly recognised his voice and realised who he was. Her cousin lived in the Muswell Hill district of London, just ten miles away; she hadn't seen him since his father's funeral two years ago.

"Hang on," she called.

Rita undid the bolt and took the chain off the lock. She opened the door, and there stood Alan with his distinctive goofy grin.

"What are you doing here? It's twenty-five to two in the morning," Rita complained. She was bleary-eyed and naturally wanted an explanation for his sudden appearance.

"She chucked me out because I found out she was having an affair," said Alan, by way of explanation, and practically barged his way into the house. Cally growled at him and then started to howl. Rita left the dog in the hall, where he still continued to growl, and made Alan and herself a cup of tea.

"Will you be all right down here if I go back to bed?" Rita asked her cousin. "I've got to get up at eight for work you see," she explained.

"Yes, of course," said Alan, and for some reason, he kept edging towards the front room, where he peeped out of the window, as if he was looking for someone.

"Are you on the run or something, Alan? Sit down and stop making me nervous," said Rita, and she persuaded him to go through his story from beginning to end.

Alan told her how he had found a gold cigarette lighter in the bedroom of his home, and that it had started an argument between himself and his 25-year-old, common-law wife. She had taunted him by saying that she was having an affair with a man her own age, who was a much better lover than Alan, who was in his mid-forties. As Alan's partner owned the house, she had decided to throw him out. Alan said he had walked almost ten miles from Muswell Hill to his cousin's Wimbledon home, yet he didn't seem at all fatigued and remained on his feet, pacing edgily to and fro.

Rita tried to reassure him by saying that things would look better in the morning, and urged Alan to get some sleep on the settee. She brought a duvet down to him and two pillows, and even tucked him in. As she was leaving the living room, Alan said, "Thanks Rita. I'm sorry about calling on you at all hours in the morning."

"It's okay. Get some shut-eye, eh?" Rita replied, and she turned out the living-room light and retired to her bedroom.

At about 3am, Rita awoke to the sound of Cally barking incessantly. The barking was coming from somewhere in the distance, outside the house. Rita jumped out of bed and opened the curtains, and saw to her horror that Cally was running along the end of the street, chasing a cat. She wondered how the dog could possibly have got out, then she remembered that Alan was downstairs. She turned round to switch on the bedside lamp – and there was Alan, sprawled on the bed, wearing only a pair of underpants. He smiled at Rita in a leering, sinister way, and said, "Come back to bed, love."

Rita was puzzled, then frightened. She grabbed her dressing gown and ran out of the room. Alan immediately ran after her.

"What's the matter, love? Don't you like men?" he said, and he grabbed at Rita's long hair as she ran down the stairs.

There was a struggle in the hall; Alan forced kisses on the terrified woman and ran his hands all over her body. Rita let out a piercing scream and Alan rushed into the living room and grabbed his jeans. As he struggled to put them on, he gritted his teeth and shouted to Rita, "I'm going to kill you now!"

While he was struggling with his jeans, Rita seized the opportunity and dashed out of the house and down the street. She turned a corner and made straight for a public phone box. Her fingers were numb with panic, but she somehow managed to dial the police. As she was put through to them, Alan came chasing down the street towards her. Rita screamed and blurted out where she lived and what was happening, just seconds before the enraged Alan arrived at the phone box. He roughly pulled Rita out of the telephone box then grabbed the receiver and tried to smash it against the perspex panels of the box. Rita ran off again and hid behind a hedge further up the street. Alan stormed off, and the police quickly turned up, thinking a so-called 'domestic' was in progress. When she saw the police car, Rita came out of hiding with tears streaming from her eyes and told the police officers what had happened.

"Which way did he go?" asked one of the officers, and Rita just pointed to the end of the street. While two officers ran after him in that direction and a patrol car followed them, a policewoman escorted Rita back to her home.

The police never found a trace of Alan.

But there was a mysterious twist to the proceedings. It transpired that Rita's cousin, Alan Warner, could not possibly have attacked her, because he had been in Coppetts Wood Hospital recovering from open heart surgery, and had lain there, hovering on the brink of death, for over a week because of complications.

Stranger still, on the night that Rita was allegedly visited by her cousin, Alan had been muttering some strange things while he was in a semi-conscious state. Nurses told police that Alan had kept saying something about his wife having an affair, and of a journey he was making to a cousin in Wimbledon named Rita.

Another strange incident also came to light, which only served to deepen the mystery even further. A charity worker who was a close friend of Alan Warner claimed that he had spoken to him outside a public house in Highgate – at the very hour, it transpired, that Alan was in fact being operated on. This extraordinary case attracted the attention of the Psychical Research Society in London, and investigators from this organisation theorised that, through some bizarre biological process, Alan Warner somehow projected an etheric double of himself as his body was being subjected to the trauma of an operation.

But how could a projection be solid enough to attack Rita? Rita said she thought that there was something evil about the impostor who assaulted her. She also said that she regretted not having taken notice of her dog, Cally, who had reacted with such unusual hostility towards the night caller, as if she had known, by some sixth sense, that there was something sinister about the man.

Was Einstein's Brain Different from Everybody Else's?

In 1955, 76-year-old Albert Einstein's health was rapidly deteriorating. Doctors diagnosed a damaged aorta which was evidently leaking blood. Einstein had suspected that his heart was failing for several years, but now the doctors were really worried, because they thought the weakened artery had developed an aneurysm and was in danger of exploding, with disastrous results. When Einstein was given this grim news he simply shrugged and said, "Let it burst!"

Not long afterwards, it did.

Einstein was admitted to Princeton Hospital, and his son flew in from California to be with his father in his final hours. Einstein's stepdaughter, Margot, was already at the hospital. At first it seemed as if the aneurysm was healing, but at eleven o'clock that night in April 1955, Albert Einstein became very pale and exhibited irregular breathing. In a very weak voice he began to mumble something in German to the nurse, Alberta Roszel, but she did not understand the language. She was upset, because it seemed to her that the world famous physicist was struggling to convey something of importance. But less than a minute later, he took two deep breaths and died.

After the post-mortem, Einstein's 2lb 10oz (1.2kg) brain was saved for study. It was photographed, carefully preserved in formalin, then chopped into 240 numbered cubes. The body, meanwhile, was cremated at Ewling Crematorium in Trenton.

Most neuroscientists scorned the idea of seeking physiological evidence of genius by examining the convolutions in Einstein's brain. It was generally thought that, on a superficial, physical level, all brains were basically the same, differing only slightly from person to person, just as faces vary from human to human. However, after some 44 years of studying the physicist's brain, a plethora of curious features were uncovered which, perhaps not surprisingly, set his grey matter apart from that of the rest of us.

In 1999, Professor Sandra Witelson of McMaster University, Hamilton, Ontario, found that in one area, the inferior parietal region, there were many substantial differences. That part of Einstein's brain was extensively developed on both sides, giving this region of his brain 15 per cent more capacity than average. Spatial and mathematical thinking are strongly dependent on the right and left posterior parietal regions. Neurologists examining the physicist's brain also discovered that it did not feature a particular groove (known as a 'sulcus') which is present in normal brains, and it was speculated that the absence of this groove may have been the key to Einstein's genius. Without the grooves which exist in all other brains, more neurons would have been able to fit into the area, in effect permitting the development of an extraordinarily large expanse of highly integrated cortex.

This evidence is now seen as proof that there were physical advantages in Einstein's brain which probably gave rise to his genius and unique world view of reality, and which set him apart from the rest of mankind.

The Man Who Led Two Lives

In January 1887, mild-mannered carpenter and local preacher, Ansel Bourne, left his home one morning in Rhode Island, USA, then drew $551 from his bank account before setting off for Providence, to discuss a land purchasing deal with his nephew.

At 5am on the morning of 14 March that same year, Mr Bourne awoke to a loud report, which sounded like a pistol being fired close to his head. He jumped up off the bed but there was nothing to see but the darkened bedroom. Mr Bourne felt strange, as if he had been drugged, and he staggered to the window to get some fresh air. He opened the window and leant out. As he took long, greedy gulps of the fresh air, he immediately noticed that the street was unfamiliar. Mr Bourne soon realised that he did not have a clue where he was, and worse still, he later began to doubt *who* he was as well.

He staggered down the stairs in confusion and bumped into the owner of the house, a Mr Earle, who seemed very concerned about Mr Bourne's strange behaviour.

"Are you all right, Mr Brown?" the landlord asked the confused lodger, gently leading him into the front parlour and sitting him down in front of the fire.

"Look here, Sir" Mr Bourne answered, "My name isn't Brown, it's Bourne."

"But you're Albert Brown, my lodger" the puzzled landlord insisted, "Do you know where you are? You look a bit strange if you don't mind me saying so."

Mr Bourne admitted that he did not, so the landlord filled him in on some highly unusual details. He revealed that Mr Bourne was in a room at the back of a small confectionery and stationery shop on East Main Street in Norristown, Pennsylvania.

"Pennsylvania!" Mr Bourne exclaimed. "What on earth am I doing in Pennsylvania?"

A doctor was called and, after examining Mr Bourne, he suspected amnesia, possibly brought on by a blow to the head, even though there were no marks or bruising on Bourne's head. Bourne said that the last thing he recalled was leaving his nephew's shop on Broad Street, Providence, Rhode Island, which was 230 miles away.

It transpired that Ansel Bourne had arrived in Pennsylvania in February of that year and had set up the confectionery and stationery business as Mr Albert John Brown. But Mr Brown's alter ego, Ansel Bourne, could recall doing nothing of the sort. He insisted that he had no interest in confectionery, or paper and pens, and remained completely baffled by the missing weeks in his life. Mr Bourne's nephew was contacted and he later came to collect his uncle. The perplexed Bourne learned from his nephew that he had been reported missing on Rhode Island and that the police had even been making plans to drag the river to find his body.

Mr Bourne remained bemused by the period of amnesia.

Three years later a Professor William James of Harvard heard of the strange case, and offered to hypnotise Bourne in an effort to shed some light on the mystery. Bourne gave his consent and was duly put into a hypnotic trance.

Under hypnosis, Mr Bourne became the mysterious Mr AJ Brown once more, and he gave a blow-by-blow account of the journey he had taken three years ago, from Rhode Island to Pennsylvania. 'Mr Brown' told the professor that he had set up a shop (with the $551 he had withdrawn) while being a little confused as to what his real identity was. All he knew was that his name was Brown and that he had lost his wife in 1881. Mr Bourne had lost his own wife that same year. As the days went by, Mr Brown felt his identity steadily 'evaporating' until it had vanished altogether on the morning of 14 March 1887. That was the morning when Ansel Bourne's ego had dramatically resurfaced with the sound of a loud bang.

Professor James deduced that the personas of Ansel Bourne and Albert John Brown were two distinct entities, with their own mannerisms, gestures and handwriting, but he was never able to explain where the AJ Brown character had originated and how he had managed to take over Ansel Bourne's life.

THE INNER VOICE

We all have hunches and a sense of intuition which guide us when we're making decisions, but throughout history many people have talked about having an 'inner voice' which doesn't seem to be their subconscious, or even a part of their mind at all.

One of the earliest references to an inner voice is that made by the Greek philosopher Socrates in 399BC. Socrates was one of the most brilliant and gifted men of his day and claimed that a strange, supernatural voice inside his head prevented him from doing wrong. Another historical person who reputedly heard voices was Joan of Arc, although modern historians dispute this.

In more recent times, the Nazi dictator Adolf Hitler said that he felt as if he was being guided through his life by a higher intelligence. When Hitler was a Lance Corporal during the First World War, he was sleeping in a trench when he suddenly had a terrifying nightmare about being blasted to death by a British shell. As he woke, what he described as 'an inner voice' warned him to run from the position to another part of the trench. Minutes later the unfortunate soldier who had sat down in the place vacated by Hitler, was blown to smithereens by an enemy shell.

Hitler's arch-enemy, Winston Churchill, also claimed that an inner voice saved his neck on many occasions.

One day, during World War II, Churchill was entertaining three government ministers before dinner at Number 10 Downing Street, when he experienced an urgent premonition of doom. The air-raid sirens sounded and, as usual, the guests at Downing Street ignored the sirens and continued to enjoy their drinks. But Churchill jumped up out of his armchair and rushed into the kitchen, where a cook and a maid were working next to a long plate glass window. Churchill ordered the cook and the maid to put the dinners on a hot plate in the dining room and then instructed them to go at once to the bomb shelter. The maid and cook just laughed, but the Prime Minister appeared to be uncharacteristically deadly serious, and ordered them to go at once.

Less than three minutes later, a German bomb fell at the back of the house, completely destroying the kitchen. The plate glass window was shattered, and long, razor-sharp shards of glass were embedded in the doors and walls of the kitchen where the cook and maid had been standing. They would have certainly died had Churchill not ordered them to leave.

In 1941, Winston Churchill had another premonition. This time he was walking to his staff car in Downing Street, about to commence a tour of the anti-aircraft battery units around London, when he suddenly stopped dead in his tracks. An official looked at him with puzzlement. The official had just opened the near-side door of the car for the Prime Minister, but Churchill had ignored him and walked around the car and got in the offside door. He sat on that side of the vehicle throughout the journey.

Five minutes later, as the limousine was speeding through the blacked-out streets, something exploded near the vehicle and the tremendous blast lifted the car into the air, so that it was left balancing on two wheels. The vehicle would almost certainly have rolled over into a deep crater if Churchill had been sitting in the nearside seat, but his considerable weight in the offside seat had balanced the vehicle, and it had therefore righted itself.

The chauffeur later asked Churchill why he had chosen that seat in the car, rather than the near-side seat which he usually used, and the Prime Minister answered him, "Something said 'Stop!' when I was walking to the car that day, and I knew it wanted me to sit on the other side of the vehicle."

BEWARE THE IDES OF MARCH

Although the Romans were the most level-headed and fearless people the world has ever known, they were obsessed with prophecies and omens. Arguably the most famous prediction in history is the one concerning the fate of Julius Caesar, made by the seeress Vestricius Spurinna: "Beware the Ides of March". This warning was made in 44BC – the year the oligarchic republic was collapsing, and Pompey, the champion of the Roman nobility, had been killed in battle. Fifty-five-year-old Julius Caesar, his father-in-law and conqueror, had been declared dictator for life, and dreamed of a Pax Romana (Roman Empire) stretching from Parthia to the western shores of Spain.

Then came a terrible omen which even made the mighty Caesar shudder. In the city of Capua, Roman settlers unearthed the tomb of Capys, the city's founder, and discovered a bronze plaque which was inscribed with the chilling warning: 'When once the tomb of Capys is brought to light, then a branch of the Julian house will be slain by the hand of one of his kindred.'

It wasn't widely known at the time, but a relative was involved in an assassination plot against Caesar. This person was Marcus Brutus, commonly believed to have been a descendant of Lucius Junius Brutus, who had routed an earlier monarchy of Rome. Marcus Brutus was cruelly goaded into joining in the conspiracy to assassinate Caesar by sixty conspirators who scrawled graffiti on the statue of Lucius Brutus which read: 'Your posterity is unworthy of you'. This message to Brutus was ambiguous, because it also intimated that he was the son of Caesar, and many thought that this was so, including Caesar himself.

There were more 'omens' which intimated that something dire was in the offing. Wild birds fluttered and roosted in the Forum, and strange visions of fiery, human-like figures were seen fighting. Caesar killed a wild animal, and when it was cut open, it was seen to have no heart. The respected augur Vestricius Spurinna told Caesar that a monstrous evil would manifest itself and threaten his life on the Ides (the fifteenth day) of March.

Caesar refused to take the prophecy seriously, but as 15 March approached, many strange incidents took place around him. On the evening of 14 March, Caesar remarked to his wife that the best death would be the swiftest one. No sooner had he ended the sentence than there a loud unearthly howl was heard somewhere outside. Later that evening, while he and his wife Calpurnia were in bed, the couple were disturbed by a tremendous howling gale which blasted open the doors and windows.

Calpurnia awoke screaming and told Caesar that she had just suffered a vivid bloody nightmare about his fate. In the dream she had seen their home crumble and had been cradling her dead husband in her arms. She begged him to postpone tomorrow's Senate meeting. Calpurnia's behaviour gave Caesar great cause for concern, because he had never known her to be superstitious.

On the following day, Caesar had regained his confidence and had assumed that all the so-called omens were but tricks of his mind. He laughingly told his augur: "Well, Spurinna, the Ides of March have come."

"Yes, Caesar, come but not yet gone," Spurinna replied.

It was still only midday after all ...

Within minutes, Caesar had entered the Senate chambers and was distracted by Tillius Cimber until the other assassins had assembled close by. Then Cimber gave the signal to attack by baring Caesar's neck. The first blood was drawn by Casca, and Caesar grabbed his sword, crying out for help, but none came. The assassins closed in, daggers drawn, ready to strike, when Brutus was allowed through. He stepped forward and stabbed Caesar in the groin. Struck with horror and despair, Julius Caesar gasped, "You too, my child?" He knew by then that there was no hope of escape. In a final act of pride, he covered his face with his robe and fell at the foot of Pompey's statue, with his blood ebbing away from the 23 stab wounds which he had sustained.

Caesar's heir, the Emperor Augustus, was another leader who consulted seers. When Augustus built a Temple of Peace he asked the famous Oracle at Delphi how long the structure would stand. The answer he received was seemingly nonsensical at the time: "Until a virgin gives birth to a child and yet remains a virgin". Augustus interpreted the answer as an indication that the temple would last forever, but at the time of the birth of Jesus of Nazareth, the Temple of Peace suddenly collapsed on its foundations for no apparent reason.

Furthermore, shortly before the temple crumbled, Augustus consulted another prominent prophetess, known as the Tiburtine Sibyl. He asked her whether he should accept the title of God of Nations which had been conferred on him by the Senate. As the Sibyl muttered her unintelligible reply in a trance-like state, an enormous meteor flashed forebodingly across the sky.

The seeress suddenly broke out of her trance and stated:

"A child has just been born, who is the true God of the world. He is of humble birth and from an obscure race. He will work miracles but will be persecuted as a result. In the end though, he will be victorious over death itself, rising from where his killers entombed him."

What Mr Butler Saw

The following true story took place in North Wales in the 1920s. It was mentioned briefly in the old *Daily Mirror*, researched by several psychic investigators, and even attracted the attention of Sir Arthur Conan Doyle, the man who created Sherlock Holmes.

In the long, hot, sultry summer of 1921, Roger Butler, a postcard photographer from Banbury, near Oxford, was assigned to take photographs of the seaside villages of Wales. Mr Butler enjoyed his occupation and was generously paid to do what would seem to be a dream job to many men: taking pictures of bikini-clad women on the sunny beaches of picturesque seaside resorts.

During an unusually hot July in 1921, Roger visited Caernarfon, Bangor and then Llanfairfechan, where he was to stay for a couple of days before going on to Llandudno. But at Llanfairfechan Roger was having a whale of a time. While a beautiful Welsh girl named Joan posed on the beach for one of his photographs, Roger said, "Do you realise I'll make you a star overnight? You'll be on hundreds of postcards."

Joan blushed. She was only just 20, and Roger was 44, but Joan kept following him around on his photo shoots, holding his photographic plates while he set up his camera tripod. Roger was fully aware of her infatuation and tried to dissuade her from getting involved with him, as his roving occupation meant he could never settle down as he was always on the road, and anyway, Joan was far too young for him. But Joan wouldn't have it, and continued to tag along.

Roger booked into a little hotel in Llanfairfechan. It wasn't exactly five-star but it was comfortable enough and quite an attractive old building. One evening he was lying on his bed in the hotel, thinking of Joan, and how she was so innocent and besotted with him. He had just developed the plates in his portable darkroom, which was nothing more than a red light, several trays, and three bottles of developing and fixing chemicals. To get rid of the acrid smell of the chemicals, Roger had opened the window, and he listened to the distant rush of the sea as he looked at the photographs of Joan. Suddenly, some slight movement caught his attention out of the corner of his right eye and he noticed that there was a small hole in his bedroom wall and that the light from the room next door was shining into his room.

"This is bloody marvellous – holes in the wall," Roger muttered to himself, and he looked at the hole and saw that the wall was nothing more than a plasterboard partition. He knew it wasn't the right thing to do, but burning curiosity got the better of him and he put his eye to the hole and peeped through. He could see a bed, and hear voices murmuring. He realised that the hole was only inches from the bottom of the bed in the next room, facing the bed-rail. A naked woman suddenly sat on the bed. She had long black shiny hair. She was sitting on the mattress looking up at someone and smiling. The woman – who was incredibly beautiful – wore nothing but a pearl necklace, and she playfully bit at the pearls as she said, "You'd say anything but your prayers, wouldn't you? What do you think – a white wedding?"

A low voice shouted back, "Yes! When your husband kicks the bucket, we'll be married up in Harrogate. Until then, you little temptress, we'll just have to live in sin."

The woman then accidentally pulled too hard on the necklace and it snapped, the pearls flying everywhere. She laughed at the mishap, then lay lengthwise on the top of the bed, revealing all of her pale, untanned body. The woman lay there, making suggestive gestures to her partner, who was hidden from Roger's sight. A naked, overweight man with a bulging stomach suddenly climbed onto the bed and started to make love to the woman. The man looked as if he was about 50, and the woman looked about 25 to 30 years of age. Roger felt like a real peeping Tom, and started to perspire with nerves as he watched the couple giggle and swap places. Suddenly, there was a succession of gentle raps on his door. Roger bolted away from the hole and jumped onto his bed, where he pretended to look at the photographic plates.

"Er ... who is it?" he asked falteringly.

"Me, Joan," came a girl's voice.

"Oh! Er, come in." He stood up to confront his unwanted admirer and said, "What is it, Joan?"

While this exchange was going on, he couldn't help thinking about the sensual action next door that he was missing through the peephole.

Joan came in and Roger had to admit that she looked absolutely stunning.

"What are you up to, Roger?" she said. "I was a bit bored, so I thought

I'd come up and see you. Was I interrupting anything?"

"Er, no ... um, I was just looking at the snapshots I took today," said Roger, inwardly seething. "Er, take a seat," and he went to grab a bottle of wine from a tray that had been left on the dressing table, courtesy of the hotel management.

"No, I'd rather not, if you don't mind," said Joan, awkwardly. She frowned and glanced about as if something was troubling her.

"Pardon?" said Roger, about to insert the corkscrew into the wine bottle.

"Couldn't we go to the pub?" Joan asked, timidly.

"Oh, all right, but I'll have to change and shave first. I can't go like this," Roger said, and he now had an excuse to enjoy his peepshow again. "Look, go to the pub and wait for me there, here's some money. I shan't be long. It'll only take me about twenty minutes to get ready."

Joan flushed red with embarrassment and coyly accepted the ten-shilling note. As she turned away from him and walked out of the room, she was smiling from ear to ear.

"And don't run off with any gorgeous young men," Roger said, and he closed the door after winking at his young admirer.

He waited for a few moments, then peeped through the hole in the wall. The naked couple next door were still making love. After a time, the obese man hauled himself off the bed and disappeared from view. It was a very hot, sticky night, and both he and his young lover were exhausted and sweating heavily.

"Come back, Howard. Please come here. It isn't fair," the woman moaned.

"No, it's too damn hot, Christine, and I've had my fun," said Howard.

Suddenly Roger heard a knock on the door of the room next door.

Howard called out, "Who is it?"

"It's me, you fornicator!" cried a man with a Welsh accent, and obviously very angry.

"Oh! My God, Howard! It's Phillip! He'll kill us," gasped Christine, and she warned him not to open the door.

"If we don't answer him he'll never go away," whispered Howard, and he unlocked the door as Christine was still screaming for him not to.

Roger was gripped with fascination at the scene unfolding next door. It was the best entertainment he'd had in years. But then things started to turn violent. He heard a loud thumping noise and a dull thud. Then he heard someone moaning.

Christine screeched and cried, "Howard! Don't, Phillip ..."

Christine was thrown violently onto the bed, by someone out of Roger's field of vision. Her face and breasts were spattered with blood. Howard's blood.

"You've killed him!" she sobbed, looking at the floor with an expression of sheer horror.

A man wearing a trilby and a brown coat came into view and seized Christine by the throat and started to strangle the life out of her.

Roger's eye, like a silent witness, swivelled in its socket, as the gruesome events unfolded next door. Christine's eyes bulged wide open, white and staring, like a frightened animal. Her blue, swollen tongue dangled out of her mouth and she made a horrible choking sound as the man tightened his grip.

"Thou shalt not commit adultery! Thou shalt not commit adultery!" he repeated over and over again through gritted teeth; all reason gone as he extracted his terrible revenge.

Suddenly coming to his senses, Roger summoned up all his courage and ran out of his room. He rushed along the landing and pounded on the door of the room next door.

"Who is it?" said a woman's voice.

"Open up! Police!" Roger shouted, and booted the bottom of the door.

The door opened and an old woman answered.

"Police? What do you want, constable?"

Roger stormed past the woman and into her room, expecting to encounter the strangler. But the room bore no resemblance to the room which Roger had peeped into. There was no one there. He was completely baffled, and simply said, "So sorry" to the woman as he walked out, scratching his head. Back in his room he nervously approached the hole. He put his eye up to it, but this time he saw nothing, because it was blocked with a plug of hard plaster.

Half an hour later, having composed himself, Roger went to the pub to meet Joan.

"What's wrong?" she asked. "You look as if you've seen a ghost."

"Oh, er, nothing, really."

How could he tell her he'd been spying on a naked couple? Deciding to be somewhat economical with the truth, he simply said, "I heard a woman screaming blue murder before, in the room next to mine at the hotel. When

I went next door to investigate, I found there was no one in the room but an old woman – really odd!"

Joan coughed and spluttered as she sipped her lemonade.

"What's the matter? Did it go down the wrong way?"

Joan put the lemonade down and said, "Did you say the room next to yours?"

Roger nodded as he ordered another drink.

"Room twelve?"

"That's right room twelve – why?"

"Roger," Joan replied, "my Aunt Christine was murdered in that room ten years back."

"Your Aunt *Christine*?" asked Roger – immediately realising the name he'd heard in the room next door. "How dreadful. Who killed her?"

"Her husband – my Uncle Phillip. She was having an affair with this man from another town. Uncle Phillip found out, secretly followed them to the hotel, and, when he found them in bed together, broke his skull and killed him, and also strangled my aunt. He was caught and hanged for their murders."

Roger downed his drink and a sickly cold shudder stole through his body. He gradually realised that he had actually been spying on the ghostly victims of a double murder! He flatly refused to return to the creepy hotel, even to collect his belongings, and spent that night with Joan in his car. She told him that several other people had reported hearing the sound of a woman screaming in Room 12 after the murder, which was why she had refused to have a drink with Roger in his room that night.

And that was the last time that Roger ever felt tempted to indulge in voyeurism of any kind.

THE COCK LANE GHOST

Cock Lane is a short curved thoroughfare in the City of London on the periphery of Smithfield, where a gilded statue of a naked cherubic boy juts from a wall to indicate where the flames of the Great Fire finally petered out in 1666. In the middle of the eighteenth century, Cock Lane was a respectable locality consisting of tradesmen's shops, private houses, a charity school, and a tavern named the Wheat Sheaf. What is now Number 20 was once the home of Richard Parsons, who drew a wage as the officiating clerk at the local church of St Sepulchre, Snow Hill. Parsons had a wife and two young daughters, the eldest of these being Elizabeth, who was eleven when the strange episode of the Cock Lane Ghost began.

Encumbered with mounting debts because of his incessant heavy drinking in the Wheat Sheaf, Richard Parsons had no choice but to take in lodgers. In October 1759 a well-mannered couple from Norfolk, looking for lodgings, approached Parsons. They were William and Fanny Kent, and they explained that they were only looking for a temporary place to stay until their newly purchased house in Clerkenwell was ready for them. Parsons took them in after William Kent paid him advance rent.

Within a few days the landlord and lodger were on sufficiently congenial terms for Williams to lend Parsons 12 guineas, to be repaid at a the rate of a guinea per month. Williams regarded Parsons as a trustworthy man, and he let the landlord in on his dark secret; he and Mrs Kent were not actually married. Fanny was in fact the sister of his deceased wife Elizabeth, who had tragically died during childbirth two years previously.

A month after Elizabeth's death, her child had also died, and the trauma of the two dreadful events brought William and Fanny – who had been looking after her sister and the baby – very close indeed. The law at that time forbade marriage between bereaved brothers and sisters-in-law, so the couple had opted to 'live in sin'. Now they had come to London to start a new life together. Mr Kent went on to tell Parsons that he and 'Mrs Kent' had recently proved their mutual love and trust by making wills in each other's favour. If Fanny died, she would bequeath £100 to him, and half a crown to each of her two brothers. If he should expire, he would leave his sweetheart a vague 'considerable fortune' – the amount of which was never specified.

The Kents soon settled in at the house in Cock Lane, and Fanny Kent gradually struck up a friendship with Parsons' young daughter, Elizabeth.

One night, in the autumn of that year, Fanny's maid, Esther Carlisle, a red-haired girl nicknamed 'Carrots', was away on leave, and Fanny was so uneasy about sleeping alone that she asked Elizabeth to share her four-poster bed for a night or two. During the couple of nights the pair slept together, they were both startled from their sleep by an eerie noise that sounded as if someone was rapping on the wainscotting of the bedroom. Elizabeth asked her mother about the strange noise, and was told that it was just the sound of the cobbler next door, who was in the habit of working into the early hours of the morning. This explanation was subsequently rebutted when the rapping sound resumed in Fanny Kent's bedroom on a Sunday night – when the cobbler was absent from the premises next door. This naturally alarmed Elizabeth and Fanny, and Mr and Mrs Parsons, and they quickly surmised that there was a ghost at work. Why it chose to knock on the wall was a puzzle. What was the phantom trying to communicate? The neurotic Fanny morbidly interpreted the knocks as a warning of her impending death.

The eerie sounds continued night after night, playing havoc with the nerves and sleeping patterns of every member of the household. Around this time Richard Parsons failed to keep his agreement to pay back one guinea a month to Mr Kent, so the lodger put the matter into the hands of his attorney, and Parsons immediately retaliated by telling everyone that Mr Kent's marriage had been a bogus affair.

In January of the following year the Kents finally moved into what they had long regarded as their 'little dream house' at Bartlet Court, Clerkenwell, but soon after they settled down in their new home, Fanny, who was six months pregnant, became very ill. A Dr Cooper examined her and noted the symptoms of fever, prostration, and the tell-tale signs of a rash on the face and hands. He quickly diagnosed that she was suffering from "a confluent smallpox of a very virulent nature".

William Kent immediately hired Dr James Jones, a highly regarded apothecary from Grafton Street, but Jones could do nothing to save her, and so, on 2 February 1760, Fanny Kent passed away in a state of delerium.

The hypocritical Richard Parsons saw the woman's death as a

punishment from God for her sins. The sanctimonious inebriate also had a theory about the ghost which was still tapping on the wainscotting of his house; he was convinced that the supernatural entity was the restless spirit of Fanny's dead sister Elizabeth. Furthermore, a week before Fanny's death, he had been terrified by a visual sighting of the ghost at the Cock Lane house, and he knew he had not been imagining things, because James Franzen, the landlord of the Wheat Sheaf (who had been bringing a tankard of beer to Parsons late at night), had also witnessed what was described as a highly luminous figure of a shrouded woman with no hands. The radiant spectre had flitted across the hallway and darted up the stairs at an incredible speed. Parsons and Franzen had both noted that the shining vision was sufficiently luminous to light up the face of the clock on the charity school across the street.

Distraught with grief, William Kent ordered a decent "lined and covered" coffin for Fanny Lynes. Fearing prosecution because of the sham marriage, Kent instructed the undertaker to leave the nameplate on the coffin lid blank. As her family seethed over the questionable stipulations of her will, Fanny was laid to rest in the twelfth-century vaults of St John's Church in Clerkenwell.

Back at 20 Cock Lane, the sinister rappings continued. Two new lodgers, Joyce Weatheral and Catherine Friend, heard the poltergeist and fled the house in terror. Richard Parsons tried to persuade the lodgers to return, but the women sought accommodation elsewhere. Parsons realised that the spook would soon leave him broke if he didn't get it exorcised, so he called for the services of the Reverend John Moore, the curate at Smithfield's St Bartholomew the Great. The curate was a follower of John Wesley, the Methodist founder who had allegedly communicated with a 'knocking spirit' by rapping once for 'yes' and twice for 'no'.

Moore discussed the nature of the rowdy ghost with Parsons, who now believed that the rapping spook was probably the spirit of the recently departed Fanny Lynes. The curate was gullible enough to be convinced of the alcoholic landlord's theory, and when he held a séance in young Elizabeth's bedroom, where the ghost was currently performing, he asked the entity questions that had been posed by Richard Parsons. The result of the lengthy interrogation was the following chilling statement, made by the poltergeist via the rap-code:

"I am the ghost of Frances Lynes, who lived in fornification with Mr Kent, whose first wife was my own sister. He poisoned me by putting red arsenic in my glass of purl (warm, spiced ale) which I drank while recovering from the smallpox. One hour before I died, I told Carrots what he had done."

The sensational accusation from beyond the grave impelled Parsons and Moore to do some practical detective work. They obtained Fanny's will and read of the suspicious proviso it contained. Parsons made the case against William Kent look grimmer by inventing another piece of damning evidence; he told the curate that Fanny's other sister from Pall Mall had informed him that she had called at the house at Clerkenwell on the day before Fanny's death, and her sister had been rapidly improving from her sickness. Moore was horrified at this revelation. Parsons then published a paper accusing William Kent of poisoning his pseudo-wife for her money.

Kent, who had been setting himself up as a stockbroker in the City as he recovered from his bereavement, read of the continuing Cock Lane saga in a series of melodramatic articles in the *Public Ledger*. He was absolutely appalled by the vicious allegations from the drunk, who still owed him eleven guineas. Kent visited Reverend Moore at his church in West Smithfield and almost broke down as he denied the "cruel untruths perpetuated by the blackguard Parsons".

Moore was swayed by Kent's gentle manner and bearing, but told him that he was convinced there was a real spirit, or possibly a demon at work at Cock Lane. The curate convinced Kent to come to the haunted house to sit in on a séance so he could experience the phenomenon himself. But Kent soon regretted confronting the ghost, because the knocks accused him of murdering Fanny with arsenic.

"Should I be hanged, then?" asked Kent, addressing the ghost, with tears streaming from his eyes. The curate had asked Kent to pose that question out loud.

The answer was a single knock, the code for 'yes'.

"Thou art a lying spirit!" Kent cried. "Thou art not the ghost of my Fanny. She would never have said such a thing!"

By now, the story of the Cock Lane ghost had all of London talking. Thanks to street gossip and the *Public Ledger's* astonishing articles, the supernatural affair had become a matter of enormous public interest, and crowds flocked to Cock Lane to congregate around Number 20, to witness the comings and goings of clergymen and reporters.

One observer of the mania was the chronicler Horace Walpole, who wrote to a friend in Italy:

> *I am ashamed to tell you that we are again dipped into an egregious scene of folly. The reigning fashion is a ghost – a ghost that would not pass muster in the paltriest convent in the Apennines. It only knocks and scratches: does not pretend to appear or to speak. The clergy give it their benediction; and all the world, whether believers or infidels, go to hear it. All the taverns and ale houses in the neighbourhood make fortunes.*

Walpole's curiosity increased as the supernatural occurrences at Cock Lane developed. More clergymen visited the haunted premises, accompanied by William Legge, the Earl of Dartmouth. Walpole decided to call in at the house himself with the Duke of York, Lord Hertford, and two peeresses.

William Legge had Elizabeth Parsons – who seemed to be the focus of the poltergeist activity – moved to another house to see what would happen. The knocking ghost went with her. This indicated that Elizabeth, and not the Cock Lane premises, was the catalyst in the ghostly goings-on. The girl was closely observed as the rapping sounds echoed around the room of her temporary dwelling, but no fraud could be detected. Elizabeth's hands and feet were held tightly and scrutinised at close quarters, and it could plainly be seen that she was not generating the strange noises.

The proceedings in the Cock Lane 'trial' had now taken on the air of a kangaroo court. The maidservant, 'Carrots' Carlisle, had been traced and brought before the rapping spectre. She admitted that she had been in the service of the Kents for the last four days of Fanny's life, but fiercely denied that her mistress had told her that she had been poisoned. The ghost said she was lying, and Carlisle shouted, "Then I am sure, Madam, you may be ashamed of yourself, for I never hurt you in my life!"

The doctor and apothecary who had attended Fanny fifty hours before she passed away, denied that William Kent could have poisoned her. Both men maintained that Fanny had drunk only their preparations. But the clergymen argued that a lot could have been done within the 50 hours when the medical men were not present.

Meanwhile, Elizabeth Parsons began to have epileptic fits after claiming to have seen the Cock Lane ghost, which she described as a bright shrouded figure with no hands. This description tallied well with the accounts given by her father and James Franzen, who had also allegedly had encounters with the ghost. Elizabeth's fits seemed to accompany her expressed concern for the fate of her father, for she feared that the authorities would brand him a charlatan and throw him into prison.

Moore became totally convinced of Kent's guilt, and he urged the Lord Mayor, Sir Samuel Fludyer, to arrest Kent for suspected murder. The Lord Mayor refused Moore's request, and he also rejected Kent's plea to arrest Richard Parsons for fraud and malicious defamation. Instead, the mayor insisted on an unbiased independent investigation into the affair at the house of the Reverend Stephen Aldrich, vicar of St John's Church at Clerkenwell. Aldrich formed a committee with Lord Dartmouth. They selected Dr John Douglas (the future Bishop of Salisbury), a seasoned ghost-hunter who had exposed a number of frauds, Mrs Oakes, a hospital matron, Dr George Macaulay, a distinguished physician, two gentlemen, and the writer Dr Samuel Johnson, a man who had long been fascinated by ghosts and the spirit world. Johnson had once confided to his biographer James Boswell that he was absolutely horrified at the idea of total oblivion after death.

The 'Committee of Gentlemen' as the press of the day called them, gathered at Aldrich's house at Clerkenwell on the evening of 1 February 1762. Several justices of the peace also arrived to act as independent observers. Elizabeth Parsons was undressed, examined, and put to bed by Mrs Oakes. The bed was the only piece of furniture in the room. At ten o'clock the investigators came up to the bedroom and waited there for almost an hour, but there were no rappings or any metaphysical manifestations whatsoever. Dr Johnson noted that Elizabeth Parsons seemed restless, and when he inquired why this was so, the girl said that she could feel the spirit tickling her back like a little mouse.

At a previous séance the spirit had signified by knocking that it would manifest itself in the vault under St John's Church, where the coffin of Fanny Lynes lay, so the committee went downstairs and prepared to make the trip to the vault. Minutes later, the ghost started to scratch the bedroom walls upstairs. The committee rushed up to the room to hear the last scraping sounds. Elizabeth was ordered to lift her hands from beneath the bedclothes for all to see. One of the men addressed the ghost, requesting it to make its presence known by a single knock. An uneasy silence followed, but the ghost did not answer.

Thirty minutes later, the committee entered the eerie vault of St John's

Church and, again, the spirit was addressed and reminded of its promise to signal its presence by rapping on Fanny's coffin. The men waited in the cold but no answer came. Suspecting that they had been the victims of an infantile hoax, perpetrated by the young Elizabeth Parsons, the learned gentlemen returned to Aldrich's home and interrogated the girl for hours, but she would not admit that she had been fooling them.

Shortly before 3am, Elizabeth was allowed to go home with her indignant father, who rejected all the allegations that his daughter had manufactured the Cock Lane ghost for fun and attention. Mr Parsons also maintained that the spirit had not performed at the vault because the coffin of Fanny Lynes had been robbed of its corpse by some curious ghoul. This claim was later disproved when William Kent permitted the sexton at St John's Church to remove the lid on Fanny's coffin. The shroud was lifted from the corpse, and the heartbroken Kent almost fainted as he looked upon Fanny's body. He simply said, "Yes. That is her," and the lid was replaced.

Elizabeth was given one final chance to prove her innocence at the house of a gentleman named Missiter, in Convent Garden. If she should fail to verify her innocence there would be dire consequences; she and her father and mother would be sent to Newgate. Elizabeth was naturally afraid of what would befall the family if the spirit did not communicate, so, at an opportune moment, she took a wooden board (used for standing the kettle on) from the kitchen, concealed it in her nightdress, and later scratched upon it to simulate the poltergeist sounds. But two maids spotted the board beneath the blankets and alerted her father. He showed it to the investigators and explained that his daughter had been frightened by the non-appearance of the ghost, and of the terrible consequences with which the family would be threatened, so she had amateurishly tried to fake the sounds of the ghost herself. Mr Parsons then added that all the previous visitations of the Cock Lane ghost had been genuine, and that he would willingly swear upon the Bible to prove that he had seen an apparition of the spirit in the company of James Franzen, the landlord of the Wheat Sheaf.

But the tide was turning in Kent's favour. He published a pamphlet entitled *The Mystery Revealed*, which contained a powerful account of his innocence, and how he had been defamed by Richard Parsons, the drunken debtor, who still owed him a large sum of money.

By the summer of that year proceedings were begun against the Cock

Lane hoaxers at the Court of King's Bench, Guildhall. Appearing before Lord Mansfield, the Reverend John Moore and Mr and Mrs Parsons were charged with conspiring to take away the life of William Kent by charging him with the murder of Frances Lynes. The trial lasted for a day, and the accused were found guilty. Lord Mansfield decided against pronouncing sentence until he had discussed the extraordinary case with other judges. It was decided that William Kent was entitled to more than the vindication of his good name. In the name of justice he merited substantial damages for the slanderous statements that had been made against him for over six months. Reverend Moore was ordered to pay Kent £300, and later had to foot the bill for the court costs. The curate was so shaken by the ordeal that he died soon afterwards. Eight months passed, and the Parsons had still not paid a penny of the compensation they owed to Mr Kent, so Mr Parsons was sentenced to two years in Newgate and required to stand in the pillory three times. Mrs Parsons was imprisoned at the Bridewell for six months' hard labour.

For some reason the crowd of bystanders who watched Parsons in the pillory did not jeer at him, or pelt him with pieces of stinking fish, or rotten eggs. Many were moved by the sight of the pilloried man, and passed around the hat for a collection. When Parsons was released from Newgate in February 1765 he was given the proceeds from the two-year collection and started his life anew. Elizabeth Parsons still maintained that the ghost had been real, but was too terrified to talk about the affair in detail. She later married, but not at St Sepulchre's. She seems to have spent her last days in obscurity, far away from Smithfield.

Richard Parsons gave a speech upon his return to the Wheat Sheaf ale house. He said it was true that he had had his differences with William Kent, but he was, drunkenness apart, a well-liked and good-natured man of previous good character, who had made nothing from the Cock Lane affair. He also drew attention to the fact that hundreds of people – including Horace Walpole, the Duke of York, and Lord Hertford – had heard the knockings from the wainscotting of his daughter's bedroom, and that all of these people had vouched that the sounds had come a good distance from Elizabeth's bed.

Did Elizabeth Parsons fake the Cock Lane ghost, or was she the centre of a genuine poltergeist case? Parapsychologists today have noted that, for some unknown reason, prepubescent girls are often the focal point of poltergeist outbreaks. Perhaps the entity at Cock Lane was genuine, but interpreted wrongly by Mr Parsons and Reverend Moore; after all, the mysterious scratchings were first heard when Frances Lynes was alive, so why were the noises later attributed to her? Unless the original noises were made by another ghost, perhaps the spirit of William Kent's first wife, Elizabeth? If this was the case, was Elizabeth warning her sister of an untimely death – at the hands of Kent? There is a twist in the tale of the Cock Lane ghost that points the finger of suspicion to Kent.

In 1850 JW Archer, an illustrator, was given permission to open the coffin of Francis Lynes so he could sketch her remains for a book by Charles McKay, entitled *Memoirs of Extraordinary Popular Delusions,* which contained an account of the Cock Lane ghost. By the light of the sexton boy's lantern, Archer watched as the coffin lid was unscrewed and removed. The body within was perfectly preserved, and Archer beheld the face of a beautiful woman with an aquiline nose. The cheeks of her face showed no scarring from the smallpox that was said to have killed her. Archer remarked that such preservation in bodies was usually evidence of arsenic poisoning. But no proper inquest was held; forensic science in the middle of the nineteenth century was virtually non-existent.

The Berkeley Square Entity

Long before Mayfair's Berkeley Square was synonymous with nightingales (thanks to Eric Maschwitz's song), the place was invariably associated with a rather nasty ghost that was alleged to inhabit Number 50, a four-storey townhouse that dated back to the 1740s. It was once the London home of Prime Minister George Canning (1770-1827), but it seems very unlikely that the well-documented supernatural occurrences which took place there were anything to do with his spirit, as Canning died at Chiswick.

No one seems to know just exactly what haunted Number 50, because few who encountered it lived to tell the tale, and those who did survive were always left insane by the supernatural confrontation. All we can do is piece together the fragments of anecdotes and accounts that concern the Berkeley Square entity.

In 1840 the 20-year-old dandy and notorious rake, Sir Robert Warboys, heard the eerie rumours about the Berkeley Square 'Thing' in a Holborn tavern one night, and laughingly dismissed the tales as "unadulterated poppycock". Sir Robert's friends disagreed with him, and dared him to spend a night in the haunted second-floor room in Berkeley Square. Warboys rashly raised his flagon of ale in the air and announced: "I wholeheartedly accept your preposterous hare-brained challenge!"

That same night, Sir Robert visited the haunted premises to arrange an all-night vigil with the landlord, who tried to talk Sir Robert out of the dare, but the young man refused to listen, and demanded to be put up for the night in the haunted room. The landlord finally gave in to Sir Robert's demands, but stipulated two conditions: if he saw anything unearthly he was to pull a cord that would ring a bell in the landlord's room below; secondly, Sir Robert would have to be armed with a pistol throughout the vigil. The young libertine thought the conditions were ludicrous, but agreed to them just to placate the landlord and get him out of his hair.

The landlord handed Warboys a pistol and bid him goodnight as a clock in the room chimed the hour of midnight. Sir Robert sat at a table in the candlelit room and waited for the Thing to put in an appearance.

Forty-five minutes after midnight, the landlord was startled out of his sleep by the violent jangling of the bell and a single gunshot in the room above reverberated throughout the house. The landlord raced upstairs and found Sir Robert sitting on the floor in the corner of the room with a smoking pistol in his hand. The young man had evidently died from traumatic shock, for his eyes were bulging, and his lips were curled away from his clenched teeth. The landlord followed the line of sight from the dead man's awful gaze and traced it to a single bullet hole in the opposite wall. He quickly deduced that Warboys had fired at the Thing, but to no avail.

Three years after Warboys' death, Edward Blunden and Robert Martin, two sailors from Portsmouth, wandered into Berkeley Square in a drunken state and noticed the 'To Let' sign at Number 50. They had squandered most of their wages on drink and couldn't afford lodgings, so they broke in. Finding the lower floors too damp, the sailors staggered upstairs and finally, by ill luck, settled down on the floor of the infamous room. It proved to be a serious mistake. Blunden immediately told his friend that he felt nervous in the room – he felt a presence there – but Martin chided him, saying he'd been at sea too long, and was soon fast asleep and snoring.

A little over an hour later, the door of the room burst open, and the enormous shadowy figure of a man floated towards the sailors. Martin woke up and found himself unable to move – paralysed with fear. Blunden tried to get to his feet, but the entity seized him by the throat with its cold, misty-looking hands and started to throttle him.

Martin suddenly summoned enough courage to enable him to spring to his feet. He tried to confront the apparition, but was so horrified by its deformed face and body that he found himself fleeing from the house. He encountered a policeman in the square outside and told him of the vaporous assailant that was strangling his friend. The policeman followed the distressed sailor into Number 50, and when the two men entered the room up on the second floor, there was no sign of Blunden. They searched the entire house, and eventually found the missing sailor's body in the basement. His neck had been snapped and his face was contorted in a terror-stricken grimace.

Documentary evidence for the aforementioned incidents is very scant, but the eminent psychical researcher Harry Price unearthed a great deal of data on the Berkeley Square bogeyman while investigating the case in the 1920s. Price scoured periodicals and newspapers from the mid-eighteenth century onwards for a reference to the ghost of Berkeley Square, and discovered that in the 1790s a gang of counterfeiters and coin-clippers had used the house as their headquarters. Price speculated that the criminals had invented the ghost to disguise the true nature of the bumps in the night: the printing presses churning out bank notes. But the theory could not explain how the ghost was heard decades after the counterfeit gang had been detected and thrown into prison.

Price discovered more intriguing references to the ghost. In 1840 several neighbours of 50 Berkeley Square heard a medley of strange sounds emanating from the haunted house: bumps on the stairs, dragging noises, as if heavy objects were being moved around, jangling of signal bells below the stairs, and the tramping of footsteps. Price read that one of the braver neighbours, who had grown weary of the noisy spectre, obtained a key and dashed into the house one night during the creepy cacophony. Not a soul could be found. But down in the kitchen, the signal bells were still bouncing on their curled springs.

Price found another thought-provoking account of the ghost in *Notes and Queries*, a magazine published during the 1870s. An article in the publication by the writer WE Howlett stated:

> *The mystery of Berkeley Square still remains a mystery. The story of the haunted house in Mayfair can be recapitulated in a few words; the house contains at least one room of which the atmosphere is supernaturally fatal to body and mind. A girl saw, heard and felt such horror in it that she went mad, and never recovered sanity enough to tell how or why.*
>
> *A gentleman, a disbeliever in ghosts, dared to sleep in Number 50 and was found a corpse in the middle of the floor after frantically ringing for help in vain. Rumour suggests other cases of the same kind, all ending in death, madness, or both, as a result of sleeping, or trying to sleep in that room. The very party walls of the house, when touched, are found saturated with electric horror. It is uninhabited save by an elderly man and his wife who act as caretakers; but even these have no access to the room. This is kept locked, the key being in the hands of a mysterious and seemingly nameless person who comes to the house once every six months, locks up the elderly couple in the basement, and then unlocks the room and occupies himself in it for hours.*

Price continued to research the history of Number 50, and learned that the house had been empty for remarkably long periods, yet the address was one of the most desirable in London, so why had the house been left vacant for so long? Had the rumours scared off prospective occupants, or had the ghost itself frightened them away? Price could not answer this question, nor could he draw any firm conclusions to the whole case. His final surmise was that a particularly nasty poltergeist had been active in the 1840s, but doubted that the Thing was still at large. But there have been many ghostly encounters at Number 50 in recent times.

In January 1937 Mrs Mary Balfour, an octogenarian lady of a stately Scottish family, moved into a flat in Charles Street, which lies adjacent to Berkeley Square. One night Mrs Balfour's maid summoned her to come to the kitchen situated at the rear of the flat. The maid was staring intently through the window at the rear of a house diagonally opposite. It was the rear of Berkeley Square. The maid drew Mrs Balfour's attention to one of the rear windows of Number 50, where a man stood dressed in a silver-coloured coat and breeches. He wore a periwig and had a drawn, morose, ashen face. The two women thought he had been to some New Year fancy dress party, because his clothes were centuries out of date. The man moved away from the window, and Mrs Balfour and her maid were later shocked to learn from a doctor that they had probably sighted one of the ghosts of 50 Berkeley Square. The doctor told them that the house was currently unoccupied, but workmen in the building two months back had seen the phantom of a little girl in a kilt on the stairs.

Stories of the haunted house continue to circulate today in Mayfair. Late at night, faces are said to peep out from the upper windows of Number 50, which is now occupied by a firm of antiquarian book sellers.

Will the Thing ever make a comeback? Only time will tell.

The Coffins are Restless Tonight

Situated in the icy expanse of the Baltic Sea, the bleak rocky island of Oesel is best known for the whisky it exports to the world, but in the nineteenth century the island became the talk of Europe for much less mundane reasons: the sinister 'unquiet graves' saga.

Upon the island of Oesel on 22 June 1844, Mrs Dalmann, the wife of a local tailor, rode a cart carrying her two children up the long lonely lane which ran parallel to the town cemetery. Mrs Dalmann was going to visit her mother's grave as she did every month. The cart trundled past the many chapels adjoining the cemetery which had been built by the island's wealthier families and finally came to a halt in front of the Buxhoewden family chapel, where Mrs Dalmann hitched the horse to a post. She then went into the cemetery with her two children, clutching a bouquet of flowers, ready to pay her quiet respects to her much missed mother at the graveside.

A quarter of an hour later, Mrs Dalmann and her children returned to the cart and found the horse neighing, rearing up, and generally acting hysterically. Ears back, eyes bulged white with terror, it was lathered in perspiration. The poor animal had almost uprooted the post to which it had been tethered. Mrs Dalmann tried her utmost to calm the horse down, but the animal reared up on its hind legs and was obviously terrified by something. Mrs Dalmann called out a veterinarian to treat her animal, and he bled the horse – which was a common practice to remedy almost anything in those days. The horse finally settled down, and the vet suggested that the animal had perhaps been stung by a wasp or a bee.

On the following Sunday the same phenomenon happened again, this time to three horses simultaneously. All the horses that had been tied to posts outside the Buxhoewden chapel were found quivering and acting strangely when their owners came out to mount them. But the same explanation was offered by the vet who had treated Mrs Dalmann's horse: insect stings.

However, on the very spot where the four horses had shown such fear, a number of villagers heard heavy rumbling sounds emanating from the Buxhoewden family vault beneath the chapel. Over the next few days, the strange subterranean disturbances continued to be heard, and eerie rumours about the unquiet graves of Buxhoewden chapel began to circulate through the town. The strange gossip finally reached the ears of the Buxhoewden household, via the servants, but the weird tale was dismissed as the slanderous invention of some enemy of the family. But the tittle-tattle about the supernatural goings-on in the vault refused to die down, so eventually the Buxhoewdens informed the authorities and arranged for them to witness the reopening of the vault in an effort to end the silly rumours.

When the Buxhoewden family vault was opened, the investigators found a chilling surprise awaiting them. All the coffins had been removed from their resting places and piled on top of one another in the centre of the vault. Three members of the Buxhoewden family and the party of official investigators spent half an hour carrying the heavy coffins back to their iron racks which were mounted around the walls of the vault. No one spoke so much as a word within the vault during this time, because the dank, mouldy air in the burial chamber seemed to be charged with an almost palpable presence of dread.

When all of the living had left the underground chamber of the dead, the vault was locked and molten lead was poured over the broken seals of the door as a precaution against any future tampering. The Buxhoewdens and the group who had accompanied them into the vault racked their brains trying to think of a natural explanation which could account for the rearranged coffins, but no such explanation was forthcoming. It was therefore agreed that the incident should be kept secret from the people of Oesel.

On the third Sunday of that July, eleven horses tethered to posts outside the Buxhoewden chapel became hysterical during evening Mass. Half of the unfortunate creatures fell down and resisted all attempts by their mystified owners to make them stand. Three of the horses died where they fell, while others became so frenzied that they broke free from their reins and galloped off in blind panic. Throughout all this commotion the chapel-goers felt strange throbbing vibrations pounding the stone floor beneath their pews. The localised tremors were evidently coming from the exact spot where the Buxhoewden family vault was located.

The mystery of the restless dead beneath the chapel could no longer be kept secret, and the people who had lost their horses, together with a mob of the town's superstitious inhabitants, joined forces and sent a petition to the Consistory – the supreme governing church body, which periodically held official hearings regarding religious visions and supernatural incidents. While the tardy white-haired elders of the Consistory considered what actions to take over the rumbling vaults, one of the Buxhoewdens died.

After the funeral, several members of the wealthy family melted the seals of the now infamous vault and unlocked its heavy, six-inch, reinforced doors. Once more, they found the coffins in a stack in the centre of the vault, and this time there were strange marks on one of the larger coffins, as if it had been battered and chipped by something. The Buxhoewdens and several brave volunteers positioned the coffins back onto their iron wall racks and quickly retreated from the vault. The locks were changed this time and fresh lead was poured onto the seals around them.

Word got out about this second bizarre incident, adding more fuel to the creepy rumours of the jumping coffins in the Buxhoewden vault. Now the people of Oesel feared something evil was at large on their island and they made further demands to the sluggish Consistory to take immediate action. The church court decided to act under this growing pressure and they opted for a thorough investigation of the haunted vault. The president of the Consistory, Baron De Guldenstubbe, went along to the vault with two members of the Buxhoewden family. He noted that the doors were locked and their lead seals had not been broken or tampered with in any way. Another witness was summoned and he observed the baron and the two Buxhoewdens break the seals, unlock the door, then enter the vault carrying lanterns. This witness was given permission to enter the vault, and when he did, he came upon a most distressing scene.

This time, the coffins were scattered everywhere in complete disarray, and some of them had been smashed open, partially revealing the decomposed corpses within. There was no way that grave-robbers could have tunnelled into that vault, which was completely lined with thick slabs of granite. The slabs were all in place and intact, and there was no evidence of any secret openings to the vault. What is more, had grave robbers been responsible for the gross acts of desecration, they would certainly have removed the diamond rings and other expensive items of jewellery from the bodies.

New coffins were brought into the vault and the bodies were put into them. Someone suggested sprinkling fine wood ashes on the floor of the crypt so that those responsible for the grim deeds would leave their footprints behind. This ingenious suggestion was taken up, and a fine layer of ash was duly sprinkled on the vault floor. The Buxhoewden vault was then locked and sealed once again, but Baron De Guldenstubbe still suspected foul play by persons unknown who were perhaps tunnelling into the chamber, so, as an extra precaution, he employed workmen to dig a six-foot-deep trench around the vault and posted armed guards at the crypt's entrance.

After 72 hours, the baron turned up, unannounced, with two of the Buxhoewdens and stormed into the troubled vault. Inside, they found all the coffins off their wall racks once more, each of them standing on end against the wall. On the floor, there were no footprints, or marks of any kind, in the layer of ash. This left the baron and the Buxhoewdens completely perplexed – and decidedly afraid of the dark, unseen forces which were apparently at work in the creepy crypt.

Baron De Guldenstubbe filed his report to the Consistory, and the only suggestion they had regarding the unexplained disturbances was to bury the Buxhoewden coffins elsewhere. This was subsequently done, and the old family vault was sealed up for good.

Haunted by His Future Wife

At a house in the suburbs of North Vancouver, in June 1996, a young couple, Troy and Stacey, were watching television one night. A little after 11pm the couple's Aberdeen Terrier, Judy, came in whining and looking longingly at Stacey. The dog wanted to go on its nightly round, and Troy reminded Stacey that it was her turn to take it out. Stacey put on her sandals, grabbed her coat, and then put the leash on Judy. She set off and did a brisk circuit around the familiar roads of the neighbourhood for about 15 minutes.

When she returned to the house, she tiptoed through the garden and went to spy on Troy through the living-room window to see if he was having a sneaky cigarette, as he had quit smoking for almost a week, and Stacey was convinced that he had stashed away a packet of his usual Marlboro Lites. However, when she peeped through the window, she was absolutely stunned by what – or who – she saw. For, sitting on the sofa, as large as life, was a red-haired young woman of about 25. What's more, she was wearing nothing but a skimpy negligée revealing black lacy underwear underneath. The stranger was dipping a spoon into a small tub of ice cream as she watched the TV, totally unaware that she was being observed.

Stacey's heart skipped a beat. She knew it couldn't be Troy's sister, because she'd met all his family. Who, then, was the girl on the sofa? She certainly intended to find out, and she stormed up to the front door and hammered on the knocker. After almost a minute, Troy came down wearing nothing but a towel around his waist.

"Hey, I was in the shower. Don't tell me; you forgot your key again."

Stacey pushed her boyfriend aside, let go of the leash, and barged into the living room.

"What's going on?" she said.

But there was no red-haired girl there – just the television set blaring out the MTV channel to an empty living-room.

"What's up?" Troy said, watching his girlfriend pulling the curtains back, as if she was looking for someone.

Stacey was naturally confused, and she told Troy about the girl she'd seen in their living room. Troy shook his head and laughed nervously.

"You must have been looking through next door's window," he said. "That girl next door ... Brittany ... she's got red hair."

"I looked through this window," snapped Stacey. "This one! And the girl next door has brown hair, and she's only fifteen. She was nothing like the girl I saw; her hair was red, and she looked about twenty-five at least."

Troy sat Stacey down and hugged her.

"Unless it was a ghost," he said.

"Oh! Get serious, Troy – don't be talking about things like that at this time of night." Then she added, "It was really weird ... She looked so real. ... She was eating ice cream."

On the following day, Troy went for a job interview at a waterfront pub. At 3.40pm that afternoon Stacey returned from college and went into the house. She made herself a coffee, then heard the gate outside clang shut. She assumed it was Troy returning from his interview. But when she looked out of the window, she was astounded to see that it was the mysterious red-haired woman she'd seen sitting on her sofa last night. The woman was walking down the path towards the house. Stacey readied herself in anticipation. She thought, "That scheming lowlife of a boyfriend has been seeing someone else. I knew it."

Stacey waited tensely for the girl to knock, but was surprised to hear a key rattle in the lock. She heard the girl open the door, and her footsteps clunked up the stairs. She put down her coffee and went up the stairs to confront her rival. But the rooms upstairs were empty. Then something even more bizarre happened. Stacey walked into the empty boxroom where Troy stored all his CDs and videos. The room had been transformed – into a nursery. There was a baby crying in a cot in the corner of the room. Stacey felt dizzy. Some instinct told her that the child was Troy's.

The door opened downstairs. It was Troy coming back from his interview.

"Stacey? I got the job! I start on Monday!"

Stacey slowly came downstairs and seemed to be in a state of shock.

"Whose is that baby upstairs?" she managed to ask. "What the heck is going on here?"

A perplexed Troy followed her upstairs. He was really worried about Stacey, and thought she might be having a nervous breakdown. When he looked into the boxroom, all he could see were his stacks of CDs and videos. Stacey put her hands to her face and said, "Troy, I think I should see a shrink or something. I think I might be going mad. I thought I saw a baby in a cot in here. And I saw that red-haired girl again; she came into the house."

A week later, Stacey was on her way back from college, dreading what she might find at home. She came into the house, which was empty, as Troy was working the early shift at the bar. She went upstairs to the bathroom and looked in the mirror at a small spot on her cheek. As she inspected her reflection, she noticed something pass the bathroom doorway behind her in the mirror. Someone had passed by on the landing outside. She was sure that she had just caught a fleeting glimpse of ... the red-haired girl. Then, as Stacey recovered from that fright, she heard a distinct voice coming from the bedroom. Someone in an English accent said, "Hello there, Lauren. Mummy's come to change your nappy."

Then came the sound of a baby babbling. Stacey went into each of the rooms and found them empty. She went downstairs and phoned the bar where Troy was working and begged him to come home at once, and told him about the spooky goings on at the house. Troy said his shift ended in half an hour, after which he came straight home. At around six o'clock, he was sitting on the sofa with his troubled girlfriend, seriously fearing for her sanity.

He really loved Stacey, and was very concerned about the state of her mind. Then he too heard something that defied explanation. A radio came on upstairs, but Troy knew there was no radio upstairs. A rock song boomed out at full volume, then the voice of a girl with an English accent said, "Turn that down, Troy."

Troy and Stacey looked at one another in utter disbelief. The song sounded like a number by the rock band Aerosmith, but Troy, who was familiar with the group, had never heard that actual song before, yet he had most of the albums and the singles released by the band. Suddenly, the sounds faded away. Troy rushed upstairs, followed by Stacey, but there was no one about, and certainly no radio to be seen anywhere.

But the biggest shock came in the following week.

Early one Sunday morning, Stacey came downstairs and smelt a strange sweet aroma. It was the scent of flowers, and the smell seemed to originate from the lounge. She went in and almost had a heart attack when she saw what was in there. It was an open coffin, on a stand, and wreaths and other floral tributes and bouquets were all over the room. Stacey's own body was in that coffin!

Stacey ran screaming up the stairs, startling the dog. She threw herself at Troy and told him what she had seen downstairs. He began to tremble and tried to argue that it had all been a bad dream. But he too could smell flowers when he went downstairs, but found the lounge empty.

A fortnight after the coffin incident, Stacey was tragically killed in a car crash while visiting her cousin in Mission City. Before the funeral, her body was brought home and she was laid in an open coffin in the lounge, where heartbroken friends and relatives paid their respects and brought wreaths and floral tributes.

In November 1997, Troy met a 25-year-old English woman who was working in Vancouver as part of a student exchange programme. She had beautiful red hair. The girl is currently living with him, and was instrumental in helping him to get over the loss of Stacey.

In early January 1998, Troy's new girlfriend discovered that she was pregnant, and Troy cleared out his boxroom and converted it into a nursery, just as Stacey had foreseen a year before. The baby turned out to be a girl and the couple decided to call her Lauren, again, just as Stacey had foreseen.

For Troy, the final confirmation that he and Stacey had been seeing and hearing sneak previews of his future life with another girl, after her death, was when Aerosmith brought out a new single entitled *Pink*. Troy recalled with a shudder that he had heard the song years before, blaring out from a radio upstairs, when Stacey was still alive.

The Welsh Werewolf

As most horror film buffs know, a werewolf is a person who mutates into a wolf-like creature whenever the moon is full. This is a myth, as most country-dwellers who know their folklore will tell you. A real werewolf is said to be a large, unidentified species of wolf which has no tail and is usually quite long – often over seven feet in length. The animal carries out most of its hunting at night when the moon is full, but these strange creatures also go on the prowl most nights, regardless of whether the moon is full or not.

Most people have heard of the Beast of Bodmin Moor and the Surrey Puma: strange unidentified animals which have been tearing hundreds of sheep and cattle apart for years, but there is another violent creature roaming parts of the United Kingdom which has also killed people, and this animal is known as the Welsh Werewolf.

Records of an enormous, wolf-like animal in North Wales date back to 1790, when a stagecoach travelling between Denbigh and Wrexham was allegedly attacked and overturned by a ferocious black beast, which was almost as long as the coach horses. The terrifying animal tore into the flesh of one of the horses and killed it outright, while the other horse broke free from its harness and galloped off into the night, whining in terror.

The attack took place just after dusk, with a full moon on the horizon. The moon that month appeared blood red, probably because of dust in the atmosphere from a recent forest fire in the Hatchmere area. But the locals in North Wales and Cheshire were convinced that the moon's rubrical colour was a portent that something evil was at large, and the superstitious phrase 'bad moon on the rise' was whispered in travellers' inns across the region.

In the cold winter of 1791, a farmer went into his snow-covered field just seven miles east of Gresford, and came upon enormous tracks that looked like those belonging to an overgrown wolf. With a blacksmith, he followed the tracks for two miles, and they led to a scene of mutilation and utter devastation, which made the villagers in the area quake with fear that night.

The tracks led into a farmstead, where every single animal had been either literally torn to shreds, or mortally wounded. One snow-covered field had literally been turned into a lake of blood, dotted with the carcasses of sheep, cattle, and even the farmer's dog. The farmer was found locked up in his house in a terrible state. He wasn't harmed physically, but he was absolutely petrified. He had barricaded himself in after witnessing an enormous black animal that resembled a wolf ripping the throat out of his sheepdog. The animal had then gone for the farmer, but he had just managed to escape into the farmhouse in the nick of time. He had bolted the heavy oaken door and hidden under a table in the kitchen, armed only with a pitchfork.

The farmer described how the wolf had pounded on the heavy door, almost knocking it off its hinges. The weird-looking animal then reared up on its hind legs like a human-being and looked in through the windows of the farmhouse, its tongue lolling out of its huge mouth, its jaws still dripping with fresh blood.

Its eyes were blue and seemed to reflect an intelligence that was almost human. The beast foamed at the mouth as it peered in, then bolted from the window to commit wholesale carnage on the farm. Each of the sheep had been left as an empty fleece of wool with a head attached, lying flat on the snow like a woollen mat. The animal had even crunched right through sections of the animals' spines, and no one had ever seen a predator do something like that before. The church set up patrols in search of what was suspected to be an evil werewolf, and bands of villagers braved the freezing blizzards with lanterns, muskets and pitchforks in search of the ravenous beast, but only its tracks were ever seen.

Seven years later, two men walking across the Bickerton Hills in Cheshire came upon something which sent them running for their lives. The full moon had just risen, and as it peeped over the hilltop, the travellers saw the dark silhouette of an enormous, unidentified animal against the lunar disc. The beast reared its huge head and let out a bloodcurdling howl which echoed through the Cheshire hills. The two men rushed into an inn and refused to continue their journey until morning.

At dawn on the following day, the mutilated bodies of two vagrants were found in a wood just five miles from the inn. It didn't seem to be a case of murder, because their bodies had been literally slashed to ribbons by something which had claws like knives. One of the victims had tried to cross a stream as he had fled the scene of the slaying, and had been pounced upon in the waters. His head was never found, and seemed to have been ripped off. The head of the other victim was found stripped of its face and ears in another part of the wood. The jaws of the animal which had killed the man must have been enormously powerful, because the victim's skull had been cracked open and splintered like a giant egg during the gruesome attack.

Someone wrote an anonymous letter and posted it to the local church minister. The letter writer claimed that the beast that had killed the men had been a werewolf which had been on the loose in that area of Cheshire and Wales for over a hundred years. He said that the attack had happened during an eclipse of the moon, when the moon passes into the earth's shadow and seems to turn dark red, and he claimed that he had personally heard the terrible screams of the tramps who were slaughtered by the animal. The writer told the minister that, to the north of the country, a farmer who had spotted the animal on the night of a full moon said he had afterwards found two of his full-grown 70-pound lambs savagely ripped apart. One of the lambs was completely flattened, as if it had been run over by a farm tractor. There were around 70 further sightings of the beast between 1992 and 1994, and London Zoo gave the farmers in the area advice for trapping the unknown predator.

Large cages baited with raw steaks and with special trapdoors were installed on the farms in the hope that the beast would be tempted to venture into one of them. The creature actually did go into one cage, but when the door sprang shut, it had somehow managed to prise open two thick steel bars and escape. The staff at London Zoo were mystified and insisted that some misguided lunatic must have helped the animal escape, as the cage was used to trap and transport grisly and polar bears, and was enormously strong. But the farmer was positive that the animal had definitely pulled the bars apart itself. The experts from the zoo said that no known animal could have done something like that.

One rather pathetic explanation for the killings was that a wolverine was on the loose, but the tracks left by the violent animal seem to indicate that it was a particularly large variety of wolf. One American expert on animal tracks was baffled by the prints left by the animal, and pointed out that they strongly resembled the fossilised tracks left by the long extinct sabre-toothed tiger. But the sabre-toothed tiger has not roamed Britain since the Pleistocene Era, over two million years ago.

From the pattern of sightings made after 1995, it seems that the so-called 'Welsh Werewolf' is steadily moving eastwards towards Cheshire and Merseyside. So we'd better watch out!

Other Titles by Tom Slemen

Haunted Liverpool 1	Tom Slemen £5.99
Haunted Liverpool 2	Tom Slemen £5.99
Haunted Liverpool 3	Tom Slemen £5.99
Haunted Liverpool 4	Tom Slemen £5.99
Haunted Liverpool 5	Tom Slemen £5.99
Haunted Liverpool 6	Tom Slemen £5.99
Haunted Liverpool 7	Tom Slemen £5.99
Haunted Liverpool 8	Tom Slemen £5.99
Haunted Liverpool 9	Tom Slemen £5.99
Haunted Liverpool 10	Tom Slemen £5.99
Haunted Liverpool 11	Tom Slemen £5.99
Haunted Liverpool 12	Tom Slemen £5.99
Haunted Liverpool 13	Tom Slemen £5.99
Haunted Liverpool 14	Tom Slemen £5.99
Strange Liverpool	Tom Slemen £5.99
Haunted Wirral	Tom Slemen £5.99
Liverpool Ghost Walk	Tom Slemen £5.99
Haunted Cheshire	Tom Slemen £5.99
Wicked Liverpool	Tom Slemen £5.99
Mysteries	Tom Slemen £5.99
Haunted Liverpool Anthology	Tom Slemen £6.99
Haunted Liverpool double cassette and audio book read by	Tom Slemen £8.99

Available from all good bookshops

For a free stocklist contact:

THE BLUECOAT PRESS
329 Mariners House
Queens Dock Commercial Centre
Norfolk Street
Liverpool L1 0BG

Telephone: 0151 707 2390
Website: www.bluecoatpress.co.uk

If you have had a paranormal encounter, or a supernatural experience of any sort, please drop a line to Tom Slemen c/o the above address.